A Book of Miracles

The Autobiography of Beverly Young Jones

by

Beverly Young Jones

Dorrance Publishing Co
585 Alpha Drive
Pittsburgh, PA 15238
Visit our website at www.dorrancebookstore.com

ISBN: 979-8-88729-231-1
eISBN: 979-8-88729-731-6

A Tale of Two Refrigerators

My parents lived in Norfolk, Virginia and I was born in the Berkley section on Mahone Avenue. My father rented from his mother-in-law, my grandmother, Martha Webb Wilson. The house was a duplex with everything being on the first floor. My grandmother had warned my father about replacing his leaking refrigerator. She did not want to ruin her tiled floors, so she asked him to purchase a new refrigerator. Because my father let the problem linger, my grandmother had the refrigerator set out on the front lawn.

When Dad returned from work and found his refrigerator on the lawn, he confronted my grandmother, then set her refrigerator on the lawn, not seeing things her way. Well, shortly after the fiasco, my family was evicted from my grandmother's house. We had to move to a project called Young Park, having little money and no other place to go. I was a one- year -old at that time and we lived there for eight years.

In Young Park, I attended Young Park Elementary School, from age five until age eight, and St. Paul C. M. E. Church until I was 23 years old.

A man who isolates himself seeks his own desires; He rages against all wise judgment. Proverbs 18:1

Panic at the Washer

When my older siblings were in school, my mom spent her day cleaning, doing laundry, and cooking, along with keeping my younger siblings. One day, as she was using the wringer to our washing machine, allowing clothes to be pulled through two rollers, pressing water out into the sink, the ends of the tie of her scarf started to go through the wringer with a pair of pants. Her scarf was tied into a knot just under her throat. In panic, she asked me, a four-year -old, to unplug the washer. When I looked up at what was going on and saw the danger she was in, I was afraid to leave her. I climbed a chair and tugged with her. I thought I had no time to search for the plug, but when I saw that her neck was getting too close to the wringer, I prayed, and with my mother, tugged as hard as I could. The nylon scarf finally tore, freeing mom from the wringer with the knot on her neck almost pressed against the roller. Thank God she was free!

Mom was so quiet it was rare that she asked for anything. She would stand in a corner of the kitchen and sing praises to God as she cooked. It was rare that she went to church. Dad would send us to church almost every Sunday, but for Mom, he thought it was a place where she might meet a man. Life was interesting at home.

On a lighter note, Mom liked to sing television jingles, usually when no one was around. One day I walked to the entrance of the living room while Mom's back was to me, and she didn't know I was there. As she leaned back on a hassock, she kicked her legs in the air as she sang along with a commercial, "Sometimes you feel like a nut, sometimes you don't!"

Through the Lord's mercies we are not consumed, because His compassions fail not. They are new every morning; Great is Your faithfulness. Lamentations 3: 22-24

Ghost Stories

Dad was a very serious man, but did a poor job at budgeting money. Every payday weekend, he would go to the neighborhood speak easy , pay for drinks, and gamble away his two weeks' earnings. This went on for years, but as if this weren't bad enough, he also wanted to fight with my mother when he had no money to bring home. My older siblings always stepped in and tried to stop the fights, but that usually didn't work. We went without food, decent clothing, and shoes, and were evicted time after time.

On hot summer nights when the storms had caused the power to go out, my dad would call us to his side to hear ghost stories. One of the stories was about his first job after being discharged from the Army. He had to clean and dress corpses and prepare them for the funeral. He had worked for several months, and was beginning to get used to the job. One particular day, when he was in the room alone, as he prepares one of the dead, a body in the room lying nearby sat straight up. My father had caught this from the corner of his eye, but when he turned to be sure, of what he thought he saw, he screamed and ran from the funeral home, never to return. He was out of a job again.

He also told stories of how, after midnight, grave robbers use to rob graves of money, jewelry, and anything else they could sell. As one of the robbers reached into a fresh grave to rob, and after taking all he could find to take, the deceased grabbed his arm at the elbow and tugged as to be helped up. The man yelled and took off running, not even getting a "thank you" from a man who had been buried alive.

I owned a walking doll when I was eight years old. With the power out one stormy night, my dad put a sheet over the doll's head, placing her beside the door at the entrance of the bathroom. After my dad told several scary stories, I had to use the bathroom. I asked if someone would walk with me. My dad said, "You wanted to listen to all of those scary stories, now you go to the bathroom by yourself." I looked through the dark, for one volunteer, but no one would help. I got up and started down a long, dark hall to the bathroom. My head down, I tried to convince myself that I could do it. It seemed a longer walk than usual, but I was getting closer. As I reached the bathroom entrance, I looked up at a window nearby as thunder roared and lightning flashed. The light from the lightning put a light on the object near the door, which looked like an extra person in the house, and my scream filled the house!

As a father pities his children, so the Lord pities those who fear Him. For He knows our frame; he remembers that we are dust. Psalm 103: 13-14

A Spanking for Rodney

I am the fifth of seven children. My sisters, who are eight and ten years older than me, shared a bedroom upstairs in our house, and my brothers, who were ages twelve , nine, and three, shared a bedroom downstairs. My parent's bedroom was upstairs also at the opposite end of the hallway near the bathroom, and in their bedroom was a crib for my baby brother, Steven. Rodney, the three-year -old, would ball his little fist, punch me, then run and hide behind my mother, telling her that I was going to hit him. She would tell me not to hit him, after I explained to her what he did. Several days went by and Rodney considered his behavior a funny game, one that I was getting very annoyed with.

In our bedroom, Loretta, the 14-year-old, had left her dress and her stocking cap, used to keep her hair in place for school the next day, on the bedroom floor. I thought about the way the springs of the bed downstairs popped each time someone got out of bed, and how Rodney got up each night around midnight to go to the bathroom. I began to plan. That night I stayed awake waiting for the popping sound of the downstairs bed springs. Hearing them, I pulled the dress over my night clothes, pulled the stocking cap over my face, and quickly stood at the top of the stairs in the dark. Rodney walked up to the stairs, head down, rubbing his eyes. He walked up three stairs to reach the light switch, then he walked up three more. Finally looking up, he screamed, "A witch, a witch!" He hopped down three stairs, then jumped over the other three, kept running, then dived into my oldest brother's back. My brother woke up and gave him the spanking he deserved. Revenge is sweet!

The next day, while Rodney stood beside my mother, he told her about the witch he had seen at the top of the stairs the night before. I went upstairs and put the scary outfit on again and came down to show it to Rodney. He said, "You made James spank me!" I smiled and went to take off the outfit.

Do not withhold correction from a child, for if you beat him with a rod, he will not die. You shall beat him with a rod, and deliver his soul from hell. Proverbs 23: 13-14

Uninvited Guest

I enjoyed talking to Loretta as we shared the word of God. When I was 37 years of age, at my mother's birthday party held at my brother James's house, Loretta shared a problem that had been nagging her. She told me that she had been battling breast cancer. I asked if we could go to the foyer and pray, and with my two- month-old on my hip, we began to pray. My son Josh started wallowing in my arms and crying loudly, unlike any behavior that I had seen from him. I passed him to my sister Carolyn as we continued praying. After this intercession, I opened my eyes to see what looked like a man in all black, until he slowly opened the black cape to reveal a red vest over a white shirt. He said, "I'm going to take someone this night!" I immediately rebuked him, but he only retreated to a corner of the room. The party went on and we were all safe that night.

Then Jesus said to him, "Away with you, Satan! For it is written 'You shall worship the Lord your God, and Him only shall you serve." Matthew 4: 10

Competition

One thing about my family, especially my siblings, is that they are very competitive. They like to be the best at everything. It is wonderful to strive to be the best, but when others do unscrupulous things to be on top, it is best not to let them know what you have or what you plan for your and your children's life. Some people love to see you down, rather than fly like eagles. In that case, why advertise your successes? When you do exceptionally well in a matter, it is better to keep it to yourself. Proverbs 27:2, Let another praise you, and not your own mouth.

I have seen the results, when people think you have a little more than they have. Rather than lift you up, they want to see your fall. They don't celebrate your accomplishments; they wait for your demise.

I hope to see many victories in my life, and also in the lives of my children and their children, and for generations to come. We have to enjoy what we have without boasting ; less envy and jealousy put many enemies against us to take us down.

"A tranquil heart gives life to the flesh, but envy makes bones rot." Proverbs 14:30

Remembering Mr. Jacobs

Thinking back, I have never lost a family member in the military, but my mind goes back to one particular story in my past. I remember when a neighbor came home from military leave to see his mother. His mother was my downstairs neighbor, who lived beside the neighbor we lived directly above in a four-family apartment. I was a 17-year-old at the time and thought about how handsome this young man was. He spent his next day at home sitting on the porch of the downstairs neighbor, drinking beers and reminiscing of past good times. As I stood on my porch upstairs, I could hear his voice and thought it would be a good time to take a walk to the store. As I passed him on the porch, he asked if I needed a ride to the store, but I told him I was fine.

When I got back from the store, three young men were on the porch drinking, laughing, and having fun conversing. About nightfall, they decided to take a drive. The porch was quiet, and I went about whatever evening routine I had at the time. Late that night, I woke up to loud knocking on one of the downstairs doors. State Police officers were at the door. I listened nosily as a mother was told that her son had been killed in a horrible traffic accident. This young man had survived the military, but didn't make it through leave.

Even in laughter the heart may sorrow, and the end of mirth may be grief. Proverbs 14:13

The Gift from Our Father

Christmas has always been my most favorite holiday, but the reason for wanting to celebrate it changed through the years. As a child, I looked forward to toys or any other gifts I would receive. We were so needy at the time; I was lucky if I got one toy. But a child can hope.

As a child, usually Christmas is more about what someone else can do for you, but as you grow older, it becomes more about what you can do for someone else. As an adult, to make Christmas extra special, I would look for things on clearance that were out of season, purchase them months early, then wrap them as Christmas presents the following December 24th. I have six children now, and doing this has made many Christmases special.

Now that I am a grandmother, I finally know the real meaning of Christmas. I know that Christmas is about the greatest gift man could have received, the only begotten of the Father, sent down from Heaven to dwell among us, then gave His life that we might be saved. I know now that Jehovah's gift is the best gift we could ever have!

For God so loved the world that He gave His only begotten Son, that whoever believes in Him should not perish but have everlasting life. John 3:16

A Flight of Angels

While living in Young Park, I became old enough to get to know the neighbors. We had moved there when I was a one- year -old, but as a four- year-old, I think that this was one of my earliest memories. I was up in my room playing, my older siblings at school, when I had a vision of angels flying in a circle near the ceiling. The angels had little white dresses, with little headbands of flowers around their heads. The angels were infant size, and for a moment, I stared at their moving in circular formation. Then I saw a vision of my neighbor lying beside her newborn. The child seemed to be sleeping beside her mother. Then suddenly, the spirit of the infant ascended to where the other infants were and joined the circle of infant angels, still flying. I didn't know what to make of what I was seeing.

I ran downstairs to tell my mother exactly what I saw, and she told me, "We don't say things like that; Go to your room!" I didn't understand what I had done wrong, but I went back to my room to continue playing. Later, my mother found out that my neighbor had lost her little girl.

Your sons and daughters shall prophesy, Acts 2:17

An Ironic Event

At five years old, my mom said I knew enough to go into first grade. I had attended the church kindergarten, and knew what I would have learned in kindergarten today. At my mother's instruction, I lied and said that there were mistakes on my birth certificate, and I was actually six years old. With my mother telling the same story, I was put in the first grade class; there was no kindergarten at that time.

I was the shortest child in the class and because my last name was Young, and we were lined up alphabetically, I was at the very end of the line. Another little girl, named Bertha, would cause so much trouble, she was pulled out of her place in line and put behind me. That created trouble for me, in that she would step on the back of my shoes as I walked, or pull my hair. My shoes would come off of my feet and the teacher 1would wonder why I couldn't keep up in the line. Her headache was now mine.

After weeks of dealing with the same behavior, Bertha threatened that she would beat me up after school. I finally told my mother what had been going on. Mom said, "If she tries to beat you, pick up the biggest stick you can find and hit her with it!" Though I was scared, I listened to my mother's advice. When I returned to school the next day, Bertha told me she was going to beat me after school. Afraid, I waited until the playground cleared, before I started home. I got midway across the field when I saw chubby Bertha and her twin-sized friend. They were both a half foot taller than I was, but coming to beat me. I became very afraid, but then I heard a "bling" in my head and looked down at a glowing tree branch. I picked up the branch. I held it like a baseball bat, then asked which one of them wanted to be first?

They turned and ran, both trying to get through the narrow gate at the same time, and not getting through. I smiled, then continued my walk home. At home, I told my mother about what the girls intended and how I handled it. Now I know that God played a big part in the results of that situation, and Bertha learned how to behave.

And the Lord, he is the One who goes before you, He will not leave you nor forsake you; do not fear nor be dismayed. Deuteronomy 31:8

The Bureau

As a child, I always wanted to do what was right, but that didn't always happen. One day in Young Park, as I was waiting for the recreation center to open, I saw a child swinging back and forth on the metal gate. It looked like fun, so when he jumped off of it, I got on to swing. At that moment, a rather large lady came out of the recreation center and said, "I know your father and I know you don't want me to talk to him about you swinging on that gate!" I was so afraid, I nodded and didn't say anything. When the center finally opened, I went in to play.

A year later, Rodney, age three, and I, age six, were playing together. We had an old, pea green bureau that stood on four legs. It had a compartment for folded laundry, but nothing was inside. I hopped on the door and began swinging back and forth. Rodney got inside the compartment and sat as I swung. Swinging back and forth continuously, the bureau began to tilt and I hopped off, but as it fell flat, with the door shut, I remembered that Rodney was trapped inside. As a child, my first instinct was to run and hide, but I thought about Rodney, not being able to get air and being scared, so I ran to get my mother. She called my oldest brother James to help her to lift the bureau up and pull Rodney out. For me it was back to my room, but I was so glad Rodney was safe.

Children, obey your parents in all things, for this is well pleasing to the Lord.
Colossians 3:20

Great Expectations

Looking back on all the things I could have asked for as a child but didn't get, the one thing I would have wanted was a stable family. One day when I went for a check-up as a child, the doctor wondered why I was so mal nourished. Not wanting to get my parents in trouble and not wanting to be taken away from a family I loved, I told the doctor of how my parents like foods like pig tails, pig's feet, pig ears and I would never eat that, which was true. I also told him the truth about not liking potato salad, baked sweet potatoes, and collard greens. That doctor suggested to my mother that she should find out what foods I would eat, and cook that. The fact was, with my father's drinking and gambling habits, too many times we had no food.

I don't know what the outcome would have been, if we didn't have to struggle so much. I have learned a lot through the struggle. A lot about budgeting, not being wasteful, and being very appreciative of the things we have. As a parent, I would be careful to give my children everything they needed.

My dad had very high expectations. He wanted "A" students, but he didn't know it takes the proper nutrition and daily meals to keep children performing at their best. As a teenager, we learned to work to meet some of our needs. Report card time was rough when you know after you've done your best, Dad would question whether or not you are trying hard enough. Maybe if he didn't have to leave school to help at home after third grade, he would have known the true struggle of becoming an excellent student.

Fathers, do not provoke your children, lest they become discouraged. Colossians 3:21

All Are Created Equal

As a child I believed that "all men are created equal." I thought that just by our mere existence, that we should be treated the same. I believed that every man had an equal opportunity to succeed if he tried hard enough. If a person failed, it was because he was lazy, didn't try hard enough, or just didn't care if he were successful or not. I believed that no matter our race, if we truly tried, we could be what we wanted to be in life. This was my very innocent look at what I thought this life was all about.

I didn't see the signs. I couldn't go shopping with Mom with a stain on my clothes. I had to scrub my knees so that they always looked clean. When we visited a restaurant after a long day of shopping, we had to carry food out, rather than sit with the seated visitors, not noticing that none looked like me. I realize now I had to always look my best to be accepted in society. In sixth grade I knew what my parents had only whispered about. My people had been slaves and hundreds of years later, they were still fighting for various rights. I didn't know that having all black children in our school was no accident. I had forgotten what the principal at the school three blocks from our house had said. She told my mother, "There are enough black children in our school already. You will have to take them to another school." Not being accepted in that school at nine years old, I took my six- year-old brother through three neighborhoods, walking 25 to 30 minutes to school, then spent the same amount of time coming back. We did not own a car, so after traveling back and forth with my mother and three- year-old baby brother, I had to learn the route myself.

The very first time I tried to find my way home, three blocks away from my house, my mind went blank and I had forgotten the landmarks my mother taught me to watch for. I can't remember if I prayed, but when I was stopped at a street corner, and nothing outside looked like a place I had ever seen, the Lord told me to turn around. I turned completely, looking in the opposite direction, and when I did, He told me to look up the street a ways to see my house. As I got up the street a little, Mom was looking at us out of the window, because we were a little late getting home. Even after we had walked that walk for a while, Mom would wait for us by the window. I know now, according to our government, we are different as a people, but according to God, I knew He created us equally, and I now no longer feel small among others, because I know my God Jehovah truly loves me.

He who justifies the wicked, and he who condemns the just, both of them alike are an abomination unto the Lord. Proverbs 17:15

The Real Story

As a young child, I was a bit spoiled, in that my dad would pick me up, kiss me on the cheek, and ask how my day was as soon as he arrived from work. Like clockwork, every day at 4:30 p.m., as soon as he entered the door, I could look forward to this. From ages three to six years old, this went on.

After my little brother Steven was born, while my mother was up in her bedroom with him, Rodney and I ran up to ask if we could go outside to play. When she said yes, we raced downstairs to go to the backyard to play. Rodney, a three year old, ran fast ahead of me and when he got downstairs he found the front door open, the screen unlocked and he pushed his way through the doors, ran across the lawn, and headed straight for Virginia Beach Boulevard. I ran fast to try to stop him, but he was too fast. With no regard for the oncoming traffic, Rodney raced across the street, and by the skin of his teeth, he made it to the median, but then he kept running again past oncoming traffic, and by only God's grace, he made it to the other side. I checked for oncoming traffic, then stormed past cars trying to get to Rodney. When I finally reached him, I held on to the tail of his shirt for dear life.

When I could finally catch my breath, I looked down the boulevard, and it must have been near 4:30 p.m., because there was my father. I thought that my mother and I were in big trouble, knowing Rodney and I are never allowed to play near the boulevard. As Dad moved closer and the traffic cleared, he signaled for me to bring Rodney across. His eyes widened, with a look of horror still on his face, at the situation. When I got back to the other side of the street with Rodney, all I heard was loud yelling about how many times he had warned us never to go near the boulevard to play, and here I was chasing Rodney across the street. He had gotten the story twisted and wasn't in the mood to hear the right answer. He told me to go to my room and wait for a spanking, for chasing Rodney in the street.

In my room, my dad came with his leather belt and yelling. His hand came down with the belt, with every word he said. My anger against him kindled at the fact that he never heard my side of the story. He saw what he saw and jumped to conclusions. I'm sure after the spanking and my tears, he could see my anger against him. I didn't want him to speak to me for days. I wouldn't talk to him. I was too angry to even explain what really happened. If life were like this, why bother to talk, so I didn't!

When Dad would come home from work, I would retreat in another direction. It took more than two weeks for me to explain to my father what really happened on the boulevard. He apologized, then sent Rodney to his room. I guess he had spanked enough. I was six years old at this time.

Also to punish the righteous is not good, nor to strike princes for their uprightness. Proverbs 17:26

Too Anxious

My chores as a young child were to set the table for dinner, or to sweep the kitchen after dinner. At six years old, having four older siblings, I didn't have a lot of chores to do. Sorting the socks for our family of nine was my only other chore, and that could take hours finding all of the matches in the right color and size. Somehow for me, this wasn't enough. I wanted to feel like I was as old as my older siblings, so I wanted more to do, when they were trying to get out of chores.

One night when it was Carolyn's, my oldest sister, turn to wash the dishes, she said she would pay me if I would wash them for her. I asked my mother if I could, and she said I could wash them as long as the dishes were clean. I washed my hands, and my mom made some hot water with detergent, for dish washing. I stood in a chair, to be tall enough to wash the dishes. Dish washing was fun, and I began to feel like the older children.

The dishes were so clean, Mom put my name on the dish washing schedule to wash dishes at least one night a week. This was fun for a while. One night mom cooked dinner late, because she had so many other chores, with a new baby at home. It was my night to wash dishes. So tired, I washed them quickly and went to bed. My dad's military training must have kicked in that night, for when he inspected the dishes, many of them were still dirty. He woke me up after 11:00 p.m. to wash the dishes again, and I was so very tired. Eyes red and tired, I rubbed them and cried, having to be up so late washing dishes, and I had to go to school the next morning. I knew then how good I had it, when I wasn't old enough to wash dishes, and learned not to volunteer for duties I didn't have.

Children, obey your parents in the Lord, for this is right. Ephesians 6:1

Norfolk in Earlier Times

Early Norfolk was a very interesting place. It was so much different than it is now. I remember when many of the asphalt streets today were covered with a design of many red bricks. When Mom and I would go downtown to shop, equestrian policemen would pass by on their horses and there would be hitching posts along the sidewalk. Huge square grates would line the downtown streets to allow runoff water to pass through, during the many stormy, summer nights. I used to try to jump over the grates to keep from falling through, but I also told my sister once that I didn't want to get on the elevator, because I didn't want to go down to the devil.

Virginia Beach Boulevard was lined with beautiful green trees that were very shady on hot summer days. We woke to the sound of pile drivers getting ready for the construction of many new buildings downtown. We lived only minutes away from downtown Norfolk, so we also woke up to the smell of tar, for the newly asphalted streets and the tarred roofs. Downtown, there was a man dressed as a huge peanut, as he pushed a small cart that read "planter's peanuts."

Almost every holiday seemed to be celebrated with a parade in downtown Norfolk. Beautiful floral floats would flow down the streets with dancers on either side. Tall drum majors led high school, college, and military bands, and Shriners with their bagpipes would always be included in the procession. Candy would be tossed from floats to children waiting to see what was next. Norfolk was a bustling place.

Unless the Lord builds a house, they labor in vain who build it; Unless the Lord guards the city, the watchman keeps awake in vain. Psalm 127:1

A Savory Meal

Sunday dinners were a big deal at our house. My dad used to get up around 5:00 a.m. to prepare the meal. Very early Sunday morning, he would get a dish for every ingredient needed to make homemade rolls. Because it had to rise for an hour before rising again for another hour in the pan, rolls dough would be the first thing he would prepare. After preparing the dough, Dad would clean and prepare chicken to cook. Next, he would get vegetables ready to be cooked. Someone usually had to peel at least ten potatoes from a ten- pound bag. We would also have a 25-pound bag of flour, because we had homemade rolls so often.

For my sisters and me, church was a must. Because my parents couldn't afford to dress my four brothers in suits all the time, like many of the boys at St. Paul C.M.E. church, many times my brothers stayed at home. I looked forward to church, but as a young child, I looked forward to coming home from church with dinner already prepared.

Before we would reach the door at home, I could smell the hot rolls cooking. The smell of chicken smothered in gravy met us at the door. The air was filled with the aroma of hot mashed potatoes and the greens were also noticeable among various aromas. We got hungrier as we walked through the house, to the kitchen. We would eat so much at lunch time, it was hard to find room in our stomachs for dinner. Dinner would be the same meal, except sometimes ham would substitute for chicken.

On Monday and Tuesday, we would eat leftovers from Sunday, my father had cooked so much. Of all of my fond memories from childhood, Sunday dinners would be a memory I remember most.

Oh that men would give thanks to the Lord for His goodness. And for His wonderful works to the children of men! For He satisfies the longing soul, And fills the hungry soul with goodness. Psalm 107:8-9

Hobbies in My Youth

I had to search deeply in my memory for this particular memory, but I remember how my sister Loretta taught me to make paper dolls, a doll house, and doll furniture. One day, when I wanted a book of paper dolls and their fashions that we couldn't afford, I came home complaining and my sister Loretta heard me. She said she knew how to make them. We gathered a few cardboard boxes we had found around the house . We got crayons to color doll dresses, and paper to draw the dolls and dresses on. One of the corrugated cardboard boxes became a house for the doll, with walls added to create the various rooms. Freestanding furniture was also added to create living spaces within the house, representing the living room, kitchen, bedroom, and even the bathroom.

They say necessity is the mother of invention. I would say in our case, it is the lack of money. If you can't buy it, you make it. We found a way to make everything we couldn't afford. This creativity came in handy for science projects. We didn't go out to buy anything. We made volcanos, planets in our solar system, and other projects out of whatever we could find around the house. Doll fashions allowed us use of our creativity to create the kind of fashions we have never seen, designing dresses we may even have wanted for ourselves.

Therefore, whether you eat or drink, or whatever you do, do all to the glory of God. 1 Corinthians 10:31

Thwarting a Crime

The scariest moment as a child happened to me one day as Rodney and I were walking home from Lindenwood Elementary School. This was the school that we had to walk at least 30 minutes to get to. We lived on 28th and Debree Avenue at the time. The walk home took about 35 minutes, so we were a little tired when we finally reached home. I was nine years old and Rodney was six years old at the time. We were fairly new to this neighborhood, and we attended this school due to the segregation laws that didn't allow us to go to school only a few blocks away. It seems there was a limited number of black children who could attend the school much closer, so in the freezing cold, rain, storms, and the hot blazing summer days, we had to walk to school and back.

As we walked to school some days, I would notice that we were being watched by two men in suits, who were usually parked about four blocks down the street. At first, I thought it was a coincidence, and maybe we were at the same places at the same time. But then, I noticed that they were watching us each morning we arrived at that particular point. Months later, as we walked home from school, I saw the same car following close behind us. When I looked back to see where they were, they would slow down a little, and would not be as close. We lived on the second floor of a house that had to be almost a hundred years old. A rickety wooden staircase led up to the front door of our apartment. As we approached the house near the stairs, I noticed that the car had pulled over and stopped. One of the men in a dark suit offered me a lollipop from a bag full of lollipops. I whispered to Rodney to run upstairs and bang on the door as loudly as he could. Rodney went running up the stairs. I looked at the grocery bag that was rolled down to half the size. I noticed that the bag was wrinkled, as if it had been used several times. My mother was usually waiting by the window. I looked at the brown grocery bag, filled with colorful, flat lollipops. I looked at a yellow lollipop at the top of the bag, and before I realized what I was doing, I snatched the whole bag of lollipops and ran as hard as I could up the stairs and in the house to my mother. I gave Mom the bag of lollipops and explained that the men I took them from had followed Rodney and me home. I also told her that this was not the first day that I had seen the men.

At my dad's arrival from work, my mom showed the lollipops to my dad so that they could both decide what to do. Later that day, two officers came to our house. One of them offered me the yellow lollipop. I didn't accept it. He asked me why I wouldn't take it. I told him, if my parents had given me a lollipop, I would take it, but I don't take candy from a person I didn't know. He told my mom that she had a good girl. They talked a little while longer, then left the house.

The men who had followed us, never followed us again, and we attended Lindenwood Elementary School for two more years. It was good to know that I could go to school and back without constantly looking over my shoulders.

The name of the Lord is a strong tower; The righteous run to it and are safe. Proverbs 18:10

A Trip Through the Woods

One thing that I asked is that Rodney never talk to my parents about our trip through the woods. It was a stupid idea that I had come up with, without thinking it through. The 35-minute walk was long enough, but I had met a friend named Vanessa, who with her little sister Rodney's age, would walk with Rodney and me midway through my trip to school. I would stop by Vanessa's house, usually she was ready, and we would continue on to school. The more company we had, the safer we would be as we continued to school. Day after day, we would stop to pick up the girls and continue to school.

One particular day, when we stopped to pick up Vanessa, her mom was impatiently combing her hair. We were running late, and Vanessa didn't want to sit still through the combing. When her mom finally finished, we had only ten minutes to get to school and her house was the midway point of a 35-minute walk. Down the street from her house were the woods we would walk around to get to school. I started to get this idea. If we would walk diagonally through the woods, the school would be just on the other side. Vanessa agreed it was the fastest route to school, so we proceeded through the woods.

As we discussed what we would do during the school day, we held our heads down so as not to trip over stones, fallen branches, and large tree roots that rose above the ground. As we continued our walk, we came to a small ditch. We hopped across the ditch, but when we got across, we noticed that Vanessa's sister was still on the other side. Vanessa and I went back across to help her little sister over the ditch, while Rodney waited for us, and back on the other side again, we continued our diagonal walk. Still watching for tree limbs, among other things, we walked a little more, until we saw two figures up ahead. A woman dressed in light- colored rags stood with a shovel, over a man dressed in rags also, lying motionless at her feet. Seeing us, the woman said, "I was waiting for you children to come through here!" With that, we turned around running, to leave the woods. We hopped over branches, roots, and stones, dived over the ditch, but like before, had to go back to help Vanessa's little sister over, then ran until we were out of the woods. Now, the ten minutes were gone, and we still had about a 15 minute's trip to school. We ran part of the way and speed walked part of the way. When we finally arrived at school, we were all hot and very sweaty. My teacher asked me why I was sweating so hard so early in the morning, but I couldn't let the truth come out of my mouth. We had all, each child, decided never to talk about it.

Years later, I told my parents how we took a trip to school by way of the woods, when we thought we would be late for school. I told them about the woman and the man lying at her feet and what she said to us. My parents, not angry like I thought they would be, said that now that I was older, I know that was the wrong decision. I told them that I would never try that again. My father also believed that the woman used her shovel to bury the man.

But as for the cowardly, the faithless, the detestable, as for murderers, the sexually immoral, sorcerers, idolaters, and all liars, their portion will be in the lake that burns with fire and sulfur, which is the second death. Revelation 21:8

The Recital

At church, as a child, around Easter time, I usually didn't have a hard time, but one particular Sunday was different. My sisters, Carolyn and Loretta, sat in the choir stand, as they were a part of the choir, and I sat in the sanctuary alone, as the preacher started to preach. As I sat thinking about the suffering of Christ, the pain he endured and the crucifixion, I wondered why God allowed him to go through such torture. I didn't know the plan for our salvation; I thought His suffering was all because of the evil devices of men. As I sat near the back of the sanctuary, waiting for my sisters, I began to shiver a little and make moaning sounds, uncontrollably. This went on for more than 15 minutes, to the point where the preacher stopped preaching to warn the congregation not to touch me. He said, "God was doing something." I realized, when it all stopped, that though I was only about five years old, I should not criticize nor complain about God's plan for our lives. He is God and everything He does, He does it for our good.

I believe it was that very night that I had to recite in the church's Easter program. Afraid to speak in front of a crowd, I knew I had to recite anyway. That night every pew was filled with people. Both of my parents were there, with the rest of my family, which didn't add to my confidence. I listened to everyone, who went up before me, knowing I soon would have to go up and recite. Before my name was called, tears flowed from my eyes. Finally, my name was called, and with tears falling, I slowly walked up, stood before the crowd crying and saying:

This is glad Easter day
Flowers are springing
Children are singing
Jesus is risen today

One old man sitting near the back of the sanctuary shouted, "It couldn't be a glad Easter day, you cried through the whole thing." With that, I returned to my seat, dried my eyes, and sat through the other performances. My parents told me I did a good job.

Fear not for I am with you; Be not dismayed, for I am your God. I will strengthen you, Yes I will help you. I will uphold you with My righteous right hand. Isaiah 41:10

It's Electric

My childhood thus far consisted of a culmination of events that should let you know that divine intervention played a big part in my life. I didn't think much about it as a child, but looking back, I can see how God was there through every situation, no matter how great or small. Things that could have gone so wrong, turned out right, and this is a learning experience today as to how I cared for my children, and care for my grandchildren.

As a child, there was always someone there to pull me out of the most impossible situations. I remember when I was about four or five years old. I crawled around the floor, hungry. At first, I was looking for something to eat, when I found a red and white pill. Luckily, I was smart enough not to eat it, but then I found a bobby pin, knowing that the television lit up when it was plugged in, I wondered what would happen if I stuck the bobby pin into the electrical socket. Well, I soon found out. The moment I stuck the pin in, the sound of regular currents of electricity filled my brain. I could not let go! The lights flickered on and off, which got my mother's attention, and she came rushing in to rescue me from the current. Thank God, when she released me, all I had was a blistered hand. Then she scolded me about the dangers of playing with electricity, a lesson I would never forget. Only God, had again, pulled me out of a terrible situation, alive.

Therefore, to him who knows to do good and does not do it, to him it is sin. James 4:17

Angels at the Game

When I was about eight years old, my brother Clayton and other older children use to play baseball on the side of the court, in an open field, in the neighborhood. I, three years younger than Clay, wanted to be picked to play with the older kids, but because of age difference, I usually didn't get picked. One of the children playing ball decided he should give me a chance and picked me for his team. Hitting the ball was harder than I thought, and I struck out the first few times. I really wanted to impress my team, and didn't want them to be disappointed that they picked me. As I waited for my next chance to hit, I prayed for the ability to run like the wind, to make a home run, if I had the chance. Well, the next time it was my turn, I hit the ball and ran so fast to try to make a home run, I ran right into a metal post. My nose quickly began to spread. Embarrassed, the only place I could go was in the house for first aid. On my way in, I could hear the angels laughing. I was told, "Don't run so fast, you can't see where you are going." Some prayers we really shouldn't have answered.

Thinking back on this day, when I was quite a bit older, I wrote a song in memory of this event. The song goes like this:

Who was there when I first opened my eyes.

Who was there to heal the cuts, when I first learned to ride.

Who never missed a game, celebrated (even) when I lost, yes my Father was.

When at last the years had gone,

Who helped me understand.

When the winning point was scored, in victory raised my hand.

When I hung my head in shame

Who was there to lift it up;

Yes my Father was.

My heavenly Father has always been there,

When the earthly one was gone.

He's taken care of me, now I only want to be just like Him.

Now that I'm full grown He still wipes my tears away.

He's on the other end, when I lift my heart to pray.

He's always by my side; He helps me make it through.

Yes my Father is; My heavenly Father is.
Yes my Father is.

Yet you do not have because you do not ask. You ask and do not receive, because you ask amiss, that you may spend it on your pleasures. James 4:3

The New President

My dad had more influence in my life, even more than I had ever thought. He would always tell me to watch the news and keep up with the things that go on in the world. Well, nine- year -old s find news pretty boring. That fact was, if it weren't a sitcom or one of the cartoons I might be interested in, I really didn't watch television. After work, my dad would also look for articles of interest in the newspaper, when he wasn't watching the news on television. He usually brought a newspaper home daily, after work.

Dad would encourage us to listen to presidential speeches, so that we would know what that president stood for. We would stop doing whatever we were doing, to listen to the state of the union addresses to hear, not only what the president was doing, but what he had planned to do. When it came to President John F. Kennedy, we followed his efforts closely. If anyone could end discrimination of black people and put a stop to Jim Crow laws, it would be him.

Dad asked me to listen to an album (45 rpm), he had purchased of Mr. Kennedy's speeches. I remember it to this day. President Kennedy said, "Let us go forth to lead the land that we love, asking His blessings and His help, but knowing God's work must truly be our own." I believed what Mr. Kennedy said, but I have seen God's work and know that no one can do what He does. I know that Mr. Kennedy was talking about patriotism and the support of this country.

I followed Mr. Kennedy when it came to the events going on in the country and in the world. When I found out Mr. Kennedy was involved in the "Bay of pigs," I wondered why he was swimming in that? It baffled me for a while, until I found that it was a Cuban invasion.

Well, I would listen intently, when it came to the matters of and where a bouts of President Kennedy. I guess many black people had put their hopes in people like Mr. Kennedy and Dr. Martin Luther King's finding a solution to the problems of voting and civil rights. Blacks had dreamed that this was the time their lives would turn around for the better. Desegregation and equal rights had become a major topic at the black dinner tables.

One day, as I stood in front of my black and white television, there was a special bulletin, breaking news. The reporter said that as President Kennedy was in his motorcade parading down the streets of Dallas, Texas, at least one gunman shot the president; he slumped onto his wife, as his life left his body, on November 23, 1963.

Tears poured, as I witnessed what I considered the unthinkable!

Therefore whoever resists the authority resists the ordinance of God, and those who resist will bring judgment on themselves. For rulers are not a terror to good works, but to evil. Romans 13:2-3

The Go-Between

The biggest regret I have had in life was to get in the middle of my parents' fight. In this case, I felt like I needed to step in, but maybe I was not the best negotiator.

One Saturday afternoon, my father came home very angry and wanted to beat my mother. This had happened many times before, but in the past, older siblings would step in, and as best they could, they would try to stop the fight, or prevent the fight from going "into overtime." At 15 years old, I was the oldest child at home at the time. Clayton had a job at an Italian restaurant, and Rodney, three years younger than me, was out as well. My brother Steven, a nine- year-old was probably in his room, so I was left to solve this problem myself. My father began yelling at mom for not having his lunch ready the minute he walked in the door. We had no phone; it would have been impossible for her to know he was coming home, when he did. I had an idea, but didn't know where it was headed. I asked my father to come with me to the front porch. I told him I didn't want him to hit my mother, and I'd rather he hit me instead. He was standing to my right side, and with his fist already in a ball, he slammed it into my right cheek. Remembering the word of God about someone smiting you on your right cheek, I turned the left one as well. He immediately slammed his fist into the left cheek. For a reason I didn't quite understand, I put both hands to the collar of his shirt, and I remember nothing else until I came to myself. I realized that I had been punching my father, as I fought on the front lawn. I was standing over him punching him, and he was in tears. I moved from standing over him, and was very remorseful for hitting my father, something I would otherwise never do. I walked back in the house first, in tears for hitting him, and he followed me back in, sat in a corner of the living room, crying because I had hit him.

That was the last time I remember a fight in my house between my parents. The word of God says, "honor your mother and father, that your days will be long on the earth." I think it is in these times, after you have done all you can to do the right thing, He steps in with His power, to rectify a bad situation. I know that it is God who makes the difference in my life.

Husbands, love your wives just as Christ also loved the church and gave Himself for her, that He might sanctify and cleanse her with the washing of water by the word, that He might present her to Himself a glorious church, not having spot or wrinkle or any such thing, but that she be holy and without blemish. Ephesians 5:25

A Change Is Going to Come

At Granby High School, the concert chorus would usually perform both off and on the school campus. One particular time, we sang in evening dresses. Of course, I didn't own one, but since I had a job, I put my gown on layaway and retrieved it just before the concert. I went to Lerner Shops in downtown Norfolk and I searched for a gown in the right color and fit. I found a beautiful floral, pastel gown that fit in the waist, but was full at the bottom. It was a perfect fit and very affordable.

On the day of the concert, as all of us young ladies were in a room getting dressed, I realized I couldn't reach the top button on the back of the dress. The girls dressing in the room were kids I hardly talked to, and too ashamed to ask for help, especially from girls I really didn't know very well, I walked out of the room with the top button unfastened. Feeling my shoulder length hair would cover it anyway, I proceeded down the hall to the stage, with the other young ladies. As I walked, the chorus teacher noticed the unfastened button and came closer to fix it. The accompanist, knowing what the situation might look like to others, quickly move in to fasten the dress. I was relieved that she had solved the problem. The extra attention was still a bit embarrassing.

Around Christmas time, we would carol in or near the downtown section of Norfolk. This particular year would be no different with the holidays coming. But when our teacher asked if we had any suggestions of other things we could do, a tear rolled down my face. I thought about my nephew, who had been hit and run over by his school bus and had to spend at least six months at CHKD, a local children's hospital. I told the class his story.

As my nephew was getting off of his school bus, at the back door, the bus closed on his coat, the bus drug him a bit, then ran over his body from the pelvis to his foot. He had a cast from his chest to one foot. He was a seven-year -old at the time.

On my job, I had purchased the largest teddy bear I could afford, to keep him company when we could not be there with him. When I took it to the hospital, he had the biggest grin knowing that the bear was for him.

The class decided it would be great to go from room to room and carol to the children at CHKD, for one of our Christmas projects. I thought it would be wonderful to sing in my nephew's room. At the hospital, we separated into small groups, and I went into Barry's, my nephew, room and introduced the group, then we caroled a few Christmas songs. Barry beamed, as he clutched the humongous teddy bear. When it was time to go, I kissed him goodnight and disappeared into the hall with the other carolers.

That particular year was rough for me and my family. Not only was Barry in the hospital for six months, but my father was in the hospital for six months as well. He rarely talked about his health, but my mother told me that his ulcers were acting up again and the doctors were worried that he might also be dealing with cancer. Not only did my schedule include school, work and homework, I also had to make time to go to DePaul Hospital to see my father and CHKD to see Barry. At one point, it seemed there was no end to our family's suffering. I really learned to pray more at this time. A few months later, my dad came home, and after months more, Dad had recovered enough to prepare meals again, and his weight slowly returned.

My dad retired because of his disability, and Barry came to our house to live for a while, since he had to stay in a cast for six more months. I shared my room with Barry, as he was bed ridden in the cast. A tutor from one of the local elementary schools came to teach Barry, so that he wouldn't fall behind his peers. His teacher would send weekly assignments for him to do. When I returned from school, and dropped in on the tutoring, trying to drop off my books and grab my smock for work, the tutor would tell me how smart Barry was.

We, as a family, tried to work diligently through all that life had thrown at us. We all tried to do our very best to keep it together, but the wear and tear of life was beginning to take its toll. With God helping us at every turn, my dad started eating more and more of his favorite foods, and Barry was out of the cast and soon in physical therapy, to get back on his feet. Our family returned to our normal routine, and I thank God for His goodness and grace.

A merry heart does good, like medicine, but a broken spirit dries the bones. Provers 17:21

Hundreds of Mice

As an adolescent, I would constantly have dreams. All people have dreams, but these were quite different. My dreams would answer the questions that plagued me, like when will we get out of the terrible situation we were then living in, and when will life get better for us? We lived under some of the worst living conditions ever. My bedroom was next to the kitchen. Raw sewage leaked from the apartment upstairs and would splash onto my bed. Since the power was off for lack of payment, Mom would cook meals in the fireplace located in the living room. To avoid the conditions of my bedroom, I would sleep on a recliner in the living room.

When I would awake after midnight to go to the restroom, it seemed like a hundred mice would be scampering all over the living room floor. I wouldn't dare put my foot down on the floor to leave the room. I would have to wait for daylight when the floor had finally cleared. At this time, I felt that only God could deliver us from such an impossible situation. When I wasn't praying, I would listen to my Mahalia Jackson or my Shirley Caesar albums, played on a gray and white portable phonograph. The song I enjoyed most had the words, "Guide me over thou great Jehovah, pilgrim through this barren land. I am weak, but thou art mighty, hold me with thou powerful hand. Bread of heaven, feed me 'til I want no more." I needed all of the positive encouragement I could get. I walked with my head down, thinking everyone knew my condition and could see my hurt. Only the strength and power of God could bring me through this.

One night I had a dream. I dreamed that we had a floor model television, and a color television to be exact. We had been watching an old black and white, and had never owned a color television. In the dream, I was assured that things would start to get better after that. Awake, I thought about the dream and wondered if that were even a possibility, in that we had so little money. For the next few weeks, it was business as usual, but one day, when I came home from school, something was different.

When I arrived home, and looked in the living room, there was a large piece of furniture there that was not there before. At a closer glance, it was a color, floor model television. I didn't dare touch it, because I wasn't sure that it was really ours. When my father came home from work, he told us he had won the television gambling. He also said that he found another apartment, up the street, that was much better than the one we now had. God had answered my prayers.

On the first of the following month, we moved into the other apartment. I had a nice clean bedroom. We lived upstairs in this other apartment, where another family lived in an apartment on the same level and two families lived in the two apartments downstairs. A maintenance man kept the lawn manicured, and the halls clean. I felt much more confident with the better living conditions. I even made new friends in the building and was no longer ashamed to invite other people to our house.

Life at home seemed to improve as well, as my father started budgeting his money and life at home became a lot more stable.

Happy is he who has the God of Jacob for his help, Whose hope is in the Lord his God, who made the heaven and earth, the sea, and all that is in them; Psalm 146:5-6

Dreams Unfold

As a 15-year-old, dreams just kept coming. As strange as this sounds, I dreamed that I woke up wanting cereal with bananas. I asked my mom if we had cereal, milk, and bananas, but she said we were out of fruit. I got dressed, went downstairs and out of the apartment. I lowered my head to keep the bright sunshine out of my eyes, then headed for the store. Near the corner of my street, I saw wide, fat feet and looked up to see my grandmother, who asked if my father were home. I thought, what an unusual dream.

My life was very busy; this was my first year of high school. With homework and chores around the house, I was so busy, one week went into another. On a Saturday morning, I woke up extra hungry. I checked the refrigerator for breakfast foods. When I didn't see what I was looking for, I asked Mom if we had bananas. When she told me we were out, I got dressed to go to the store. Leaving the apartment building, the sun was so bright I put my hand to my forehead to block the sun, then looked down to keep the sun out of my eyes. As I walked in the direction of the store, I kept my head down, but as I drew near to the corner, I met some wide, black, runover shoes and I knew those feet belonged to my grandmother. I looked up and she asked, "Where is your father?" I told her I would take her to him. Inside the house, I called my father to the living room and my grandmother told him that his father had passed away. We all stood in tears.

The Dreams Continue

It was very important to have my own money as a teenager. I hated to ask my parents constantly for money, so I thought I'd get a job. I was only 15 years old, and knowing I had to be at least 16 to get a job, I lied about my age. I applied for a job at a nearby department store and when my application was accepted, I was given a math test, and started working very shortly after the day I had applied. Other teens worked for this company, but they worked nights from 5:30 pm until 9:30 pm. Those also were my hours. Finally, I had my own money, no longer having to rely totally on my parents. My station on the job was to pop popcorn and to sell chocolates by the pound or whatever amount the customer wanted to purchase. I also measured and cut fabric for customers, who were into sewing and making their own fashions. The thing I hated about the job was going home alone on dark streets. I didn't feel very safe.

As I slept one night, I had the strangest dream. I dreamed a lady comes into the store, looks around a bit, then walks over to my counter. After looking back and forth through the album racks, she asks, "Do you have the album, Jesus Christ Superstar?" Well, I thought, what a weird dream. Now I'm dreaming about being at work, even when I'm sleeping.

Weeks went by, and one day while standing around in the store with nothing much to do, feeling a little hungry, I saw a piece of chocolate out of the bin, popped it in my mouth, then turned to the front of the store, because we shouldn't have been eating during work hours. As I stood facing the front of the store, a lady came through the door. She was dressed in a fitting striped blouse, olive green stretch pants, and her blonde hair was cut in a bob. This was the lady from my dream. My eyes stayed on her as she searched the front of the store for something, but when she couldn't find it, she walked over to my counter. She flipped back and forth through the box of albums we had left, but when she didn't find what she was looking for, she came to me and asked, "Do you have the album, Jesus Christ Superstar?" My eyes widened, my mouth fell open , and my hand cupped my mouth! A few seconds later, I was able to let her know that we were out. She must have thought I was the strangest person she had ever met. My dreams were getting a little frightening.

What Dreams We Dream

Working at the department store afforded me the opportunity to meet many new people. I acquainted myself with people of all ages. Some people worked on the sale's floor; we would interact almost every day I worked. Some people worked in the office upstairs, and still others spent much of their time in the stockroom, checking in freight and doing other duties. I would always work on the sales floor, so usually the store was a very busy place.

I would rarely talk to the elderly lady, who worked in the stockroom. She was friendly, but she preferred the isolation of the stockroom, because it was the quietest place in the store to work. I would speak to her in passing, but rarely got to interact with her. Many of the other workers got to know me as we would have Christmas parties and other celebrations off the job.

I experienced an unusual dream one night. An elderly woman with a broom or mop handle in her hand was chasing a small animal around the house. The area of the room was very small. The chairs in the room seem very close in proximity, and a hassock sat in the middle of the floor. Suddenly, she trips as she attempts to pass the hassock. The wooden handle moves towards her face, then an eyeball rolls across the floor. I immediately woke up in tears. I sat on the side of my bed for about 30 minutes, then got dressed to go to my sister Carolyn's house to tell her about the dream.

I walked to Carolyn's house, which was about six blocks from where we lived, but when I told her the dream, she laughed and said, "things like that doesn't really happen." I thought about it again, and thought maybe she was right. Because I dream something, doesn't mean it will happen. I talked to her for a while, read a few books to her children, then went home to prepare for work. Weeks went by and it was business as usual, nothing out of the ordinary happened.

One afternoon, I came in the back door of the store, because I was running late, and probably because I got a ride that particular day. Entering the door, Mary, one of the salesclerks, had a card in her hand. She said she wanted me to sign the card and she was raising money for the elderly stock clerk, who had an accident chasing a pet in her apartment. I signed the card and rushed to clock-in. With tears falling down my face, I remembered the dream.

And it shall come to pass in the last days, says God, that I will pour out of My Spirit on all flesh; Your sons and daughters shall prophesy, Your young men shall see visions, Your old men shall dream dreams. Acts 2:17

The Crush

As a 15-year-old, working at a department store, I had encountered many people that I worked with, and many people just passing through. We had many managers and assistant managers from time to time, as years passed by. They seemed to only stay for a year or two, then seek work elsewhere. Up until this particular time, the managers were older white men, but as I was busy at my counter one evening, down from the office came a very handsome man, a little older than 30 years. The first black manager I had ever seen at the store. I was infatuated.

At home that night, I got my sketch pad out and began to draw, not knowing what the results would be. By the time I completed my work, there was a colored outline of what looked like a lion. On the paper, I wrote the name Mr. Bailey and taped the drawing to my bedroom wall. Each morning I woke up, the first thing I looked at, was the cartoon drawing of Mr. Bailey.

A few weeks later, I got up the nerve to show him the picture. He said, "Very cute, can I have it to take home?" Of course, I said yes, and I went on with my work. When I look back today, I realize that was the only crush that I can remember. Mr. Bailey probably took the drawing home to show to his wife, and told her what a sweet kid I was. I quickly got over it, and it was back to school and work.

For all that is in the world—the lust of the flesh, the lust of the eyes, and the pride of life—is not of the Father but is of the world. And the world is passing away and the lusts of it; 1 John 2:16

Integration and Busing

My most memorable day of school was the day I was bused to Granby High School. Busing was used to stop segregation, and to achieve a racial balance in the school system. I thought it would be no big deal, since I had attended Blair Junior High School and the blacks and white students had no problems there. It couldn't be much different attending high school. As in each first day of school, I was very anxious to see what the new school would be like. I prepared my clothes the night before and was so excited, I could hardly sleep.

In the morning, I walked over two streets to the corner, where the bus would come. The bus was crowded with students from the Huntersville section of Norfolk. We lived in the Park Place section, and this already sounded like an accident waiting to happen, because the boys in these two places didn't get along. On the trip to school, the students got a little loud in their conversations, with first day of school excitement. The bus driver continuously asked them to lower their voices. It seemed the closer we got to school, the louder the students became, until the driver threatened to take us to jail, instead of to school.

Reaching the street on the side of the school building, I noticed the many colorful messages in the street. The messages expressed that we were not wanted at the school and we should go home. There were many threats about what a certain group of students will do to us, should we stay. This was different from any school that I had gone to. Who would allow these kinds of messages on school property? The sad thing about it was the writing remained in the streets for weeks. I began to think that no one wanted us at this new school. I wondered what kinds of teachers and staff were at this new school. I was a bit terrified of what I might find out.

At lunch, a teacher by the name of Mr. Carrington, a black teacher, greeted the new students. He had taught at Booker T. Washington High, and now he was teaching at Granby High. I told him that three of my older siblings had attended Booker T. and he asked their names. When I mentioned my sister Carolyn, he said he remembered her. She sang in the choir there and I'm sure she had several solo parts. When I told Carolyn, Mr. Carrington was at Granby High, she remembered him as well, probably because he was always smiling and didn't let life's situations get him down.

Many teachers there were very kind, both young and old. My art teacher was in her twenties and would help her students in any way she could. She also admired my artwork, which helped me to decide on a career. My music teacher was in his early thirties, as far as I could tell, and had a very pleasant personality. He was always kind, until it was almost time for a concert, and we hadn't yet mastered all of the words to a song or all of the notes. I was a member of the concert chorus. My literature teacher, the one who taught me to appreciate Shakespeare, was a very stern, but very kind, older lady, who applauded me when I recited the soliloquy, "To be, or not to be." There was one teacher I found to be unkind. He would say things like, "We have two of them in this class and both of them have the same name. Not only do they all look alike, they are all named the same." He would sleep during class, head on the desk, and would teach very little. He is sometimes seen near a bar near the zoological park on Granby Street. I thought if I could get through his class, I could get through anything.

As we traveled to and from school, especially in the morning, the bus driver would continuously threaten to take us to jail. We were late for school most of the time, as the bus was redirected towards the city hall jail, opposite the trip to school. Breakfast and lunch were free for low-income families, but we never made it to school for breakfast. When we got to school, we would pick up a tardy note from the office, then proceeded to class.

Integration affords us the opportunity to discover who we are, as a people. Most people you would want to get to know because of their kind hearts. There are some people you will never get to really know, because they don't want to get to know you. They have already decided, without really knowing you, who you are. These people will never befriend you, nor want you as an acquaintance.

A man who has friends must himself be friendly, but there is a friend who sticks closer than a brother. Proverbs 18:24

The Painting

Painting gave me a chance to express who I am, while giving me the opportunity to work in my quiet space and be me. I sometimes, just want to be in a quiet place, where I don't have to talk to others, though they are working around me, and sort out my life. Though this was my second experience painting, the first was a watercolor painting of some flowers, this tempera painting was demanding all of my attention for this new project I was now working on. The assignment was to take a small square of a photograph, given by the teacher, glue it to a large white piece of sketching paper, and use the paint to make the square photo blend in without putting any paint on the photo. Because I loved a challenge, I spent my week in the class engrossed in that project.

The project was more difficult than I thought. The picture reminded me of the foam flowing from a mug of beer. My father and older brothers were beer drinkers, so imagining foam spilling over and down a glass, I glued the photo where it would best fit in the picture. Knowing also that the foam wouldn't add enough color to add interest to the finished painting, I put a lemon on one side, just for its bright yellow color. With this, I worked diligently, applying color with a sponge and using several different colors to create the allusion of looking at foam. As I worked, the vice principal wandered in the class, looking over the shoulder of a select group of students as we worked. After looking over my shoulder as I painted, she went back to the teacher and said, "Those nigras do all right, don't they?" The teacher nodded in agreement, and the vice principal continued walking around, observing students as we painted.

After a couple of weeks, the painting was finished. I had achieved what I set out to do. I had created a glass of beer, with foam rising, then spilling down the side of the glass, and the bright yellow lemon added additional interest to the painting. No matter how you turned the painting, the photo that was glued to the paper and never touched by my paint, was not noticed in the picture. I received an "A" for my effort, and the painting was placed in the showcase outside, where many of my finished projects were displayed after completion. Many of the art students had found this task too difficult to do, but it challenged me, and gave me the space to sort out my life, as I worked.

When the painting was finally removed from the showcase and it was time to take it home, I proudly showed it to passersby. It was a very hot day. I stopped at a local confectioner, near my house, for a soda. When the store owner saw the painting, he was entranced. He mentioned that he sold beer and he would love the painting for his store. Proud that he would put up a picture that I had painted, I gave him the painting. It never made it home for my parents to see. The store owner proudly displayed the painting, which remained in the store for many years, until the store finally closed.

You shall make no other gods before Me. You shall not make for yourself a carved image—any likeness of anything that is in heaven above, or that is in the earth beneath, or that is in the water under the earth; you shall not bow down to them nor serve them. For I, the Lord your God, am a jealous God, visiting the iniquity of the fathers upon the children to the third and fourth generations of those who hate Me, but showing mercy to thousands, to those who love Me and keep My commandments. Exodus 20:4

First College Year

Eighteen years old now, it is back in school for my first year of college. I thought this was just an extension of high school. I was given syllabuses from all of the classes with coursework that was due at various times. I thought that should be pretty easy. On weekends, my friends Edith and Regina, friends I made years before when our family lived in the apartment next door to their family, went to a club for a night of dancing at Fort Story at least three times out of a month. They worked, rather than attended college, after high school. Well, Regina married and had a child, so she spent much of her time at home. I still held my part- time job and continued chores around the house. My life was getting more hectic than I had thought it would be. Something had to give.

Sitting at the club, trying to hang out with my friend, I would fall asleep at the table, between drinks and dances. I would feel my elbow slowly sliding to one side until it was off the table and I would wake up. Soon I had enough of going out just to be out, and stayed at home.

At school, it was pretty much the same. I was falling asleep at the desk during a lecture, my arm that held up my head, began to slide off of my desk, and when it went off of the edge, I woke up. My notes looked like I was reading the rhythm of a patient with a bad heart. As I slowly crept into a sleep that got deeper and deeper, the lines on my paper went from jagged to a straight line. At home, trying to read my notes, I found it was easier to reread the information, than to count on notes from the lecture. Since my brother had paid for my first semester, I didn't want to disappoint him, nor myself, with unacceptable grades. I had to work harder. I couldn't afford to give up work, but the weekend night life had to go. I didn't have time, nor money, to retake the same classes.

Wisdom is the principal thing; Therefore get wisdom. And in all your getting, get understanding. Exalt her, and she will bring you honor, when you embrace her. She will place on your head an ornament of grace; A crown of glory she will deliver to you. Proverbs 4:7-9

First Time Lyricist

When my family moved into the four-family apartment, I acquainted myself more with my downstairs neighbor, Geraldine. It wasn't my first time meeting her, but because of our age difference, we never really sat down for a conversation. As we got to know each other more, and had shared interests, we spent more and more time together discussing problems, interests, and even people we might want to date someday. I also found that she was an avid Michael Jackson fan and possibly a part of his fan club. I liked listening to the Jackson Five, but wasn't as wrapped up in their lives as she had seemed to be. When she asked which brother I would date if I had the opportunity, I told her I would date Jackie because of his age.

As time went on, Geraldine asked me if I would write a song for the Jackson Five, or maybe she said Michael. I thought about it and since I was at her house, when I went upstairs to mine, I began to write. I wrote the song as if it were about two friends, and it went like this:

Ben the two of us need look no more;
We both found what we were looking for.
With a friend to call my own,
I'll never be alone, and you my friend will see
You've got a friend in me.

Ben you're always roaming here and there,
You feel you're not wanted anywhere,
If you ever looked behind and don't like what you find
There's something you should know,
You've got a place to go.

I gave this to Geraldine to submit to the Jacksons, but a few weeks later, she told me it was too short. They said they needed more. I asked what the song was supposed to be about, anyway. When she said a rat, I thought maybe the song was something they couldn't use. Well, I added another verse:
Ben most people would turn you away,

I don't listen to a word they say;
They don't see you as I do,
I wish they would try to;
I'm sure they'd think again,
If they had a friend like Ben.

Well, Geraldine submitted this to the Jackson family, and I didn't hear any more about it. The first time I heard the song again was when I watched the movie *Ben,* and heard Michael singing the song. At that time, I didn't know the financial stability that could come from such work. I was just a friend trying to look out for another friend. At 17 years old, this would have been pretty lucrative work.

Do not rob the poor because he is poor, nor oppress the afflicted in the gate; For the Lord will plead their cause, and plunder the soul of those who plunder them. Proverbs 22:22-23

The Strangers

College was interesting enough with the regular classes, but there was a class that was required for us to take for three years, for no credit. As if that were not enough, the class required the students to stand toe to toe in front of each other, and explore the other student through, hopefully, innocent touches. The lights were out during these short sessions, but I have to wonder what the instructor could have been thinking to come up with this idea. The class was held from 5:30-6:30 p.m., and on winter nights, by the time I got out of class and arrived at the bus stop, the last bus for this area would have departed.

After class one winter night, I waited and waited for a bus near the college. No bus in sight, a man walked over and said that the last bus for the area had gone already. Realizing that I would have to take a second bus downtown, and I would be very late getting home, I turned to walk to a different stop for a different bus a few blocks away. The man stated that he didn't mind giving me a ride, since the bus has left, and I asked, "Are you sure you don't mind and will it take you out of your way?" He said that he didn't mind, and when I told him the area I was heading, he said he was going in that direction. Against my better judgment, I got in this older modeled car. Once I was in the car, another middle-aged man sat in the front seat with me and the driver. I didn't even know where the man had come from. Suddenly there was a glow around me only. The driver seemed to be listening to something I didn't hear. He told me he had to take me home. He said other girls, who got in the car, he didn't take home.

I didn't speak to these men all the way back to my neighborhood, except to give them a fake name. I had them drop me off a few blocks away from my house, and when they drove away, I ran to my house. Thank God for protecting me, when I was not as cautious, as I know I should have been.

Better is the poor who walks in integrity than one perverse in his ways, though he be rich. Proverbs 28:6

No More School

My yearbook, although I can't find it around the house at this time, would tell you that I graduated from high school with the class of 1972, with no honors. It would display a picture of me among the singers in the concert chorus. Although some parents had spent their extra dollars to show what their child looked like, when the child was a cuddly baby, no picture like that could be found of me. At the end of each school year, I celebrated my birthday, and I was about to be free of school, the celebration of celebrations! I would be 18 years old, get to work a full-time job, and buy clothes that I couldn't afford before. Get the most stylish shoes to match my outfits. Endless opportunities awaited. The possibilities were more exciting than graduation!

Shortly after graduation, my oldest brother James came to visit. He asked, "Beverly, now that you have graduated high school, what do you plan to do with your life?" My answer was, "I don't know." He asked, "Do you plan to go to college?" Of course, the answer was no, I couldn't work full time and go to college, but he was so excited at the thought, I couldn't tell him what my plans were. Then he said, "You don't want to date and have children, like other girls, surely you want to go to college," and I thought, "Nooooooooo! " But I wouldn't tell him that. He was my oldest brother. Well, he went on, "Have you applied for grants or loans so that you can go to school?" I thought, "Why do I need to pay for what I don't want to do?" He told me that since it was too late to apply for grants and loans for the upcoming semester, he would pay for the first semester. I really hadn't planned to go back to school, but I said, "thank you," and I thought I had better prepare for college. Because it was too late to secure financial aid for the first semester, my brother paid the cost, and when college started, I was an art major like my brother was, at Norfolk State College.

Apply your heart to instruction, and your ears to words of knowledge. Proverbs 24:12

"To Sleep Perchance to Dream"

At the age of 19 years, I would still spend a few weekend nights at the club at Fort Story with my friend Edith, usually. This was rare, because I still was in college and I still had an evening job. Edith's mother had purchased a car for her, and with my giving her gas money, we would venture to the club at Fort Story from time to time. I found myself too tired to go many times, but went only because it was Saturday night.

I would bring money for the drinks I ordered, because I didn't want to feel obligated to dance with nor talk to any one particular young man, nor did I want a stranger following us on the ride home. I wanted to be committed to nobody at that time, and paying my own way, to me, was the answer. We went to have fun, and return home.

My mom gave me a midnight curfew that I was always breaking. The club didn't open until around 11:00 p.m., and the trip took about 30 minutes from our house. Edith and I would get back to our houses at about 1:00 or 2:00 a.m. I would take off my shoes to quietly walk in, while everyone in the house slept. There were nights when the living room light was on when I returned home late, and I knew I was in big trouble with my mom.

Regina married her high school sweetheart, and had a child immediately following high school. She still wanted to party with us at Fort Story. She lived at her mother's house as well. Each week, one of the girls would call me with their invitation to the club, and more and more I would decline.

At 22 years old, I had met and married my husband. It was game over for hanging out with my friends. I didn't want him to have a reason to think that I was an unfaithful wife. My husband was stationed aboard the USS John F. Kennedy in Norfolk, and was on a six- month deployment at this particular time. I spent most of my time working and staying home, though the first year we were married, we lived with my parents for reasons I will discuss later.

On a night that I came home from work, very tired after having worked six nights that week, getting home at about 10:00 p.m., I was in bed when the phone rang. It was Regina, wanting me to keep her little girl, while she went to the club. Although she was married also, at this time, she was separated, and just wanted to go out. I told her I was just too tired to babysit, and I was already in bed. She asked if I could just put the little girl beside me and continue sleeping, but I told her I was just too tired. I got off of the phone and went back to bed.

I had babysat for Regina's little girl several times before, and she, being almost two years old at the time, would call me Bluh Bluh, because Beverly was too hard to say. When her mom had to work or go out, she would tell her mom, "I want to go to Bluh Bluh's house."

As I slept the night of the call from Regina, sometime in the middle of the night, I had a strange experience, an out-of-body experience. I sat up, but my body was still lying in bed asleep. As I sat up looking out of my bedroom window at a church that was directly across from the apartment, I could hear the voice of a little girl; it was Regina's little girl. A man asked her where she was going and she said, "I'm going to Bluh Bluh's house." In my mind I could see her walking, holding a little receiving blanket, as she stopped in front of our apartment building, then went down the street and around the corner. Having no control of my body, my spirit, I think, reclined back down to my body, and I continued sleeping. I slept until the constant ringing of the telephone disturbed that sleep. My dad yelled from his bedroom down the hall, "Beverly, get up; you know the phone is for you. It is probably your husband calling from overseas!" I finally got up to answer the phone, but it was Regina, looking for her little girl, at 3:00 a.m. I told her she was not with me; I was asleep in my bed. I quickly got dressed and we both searched the streets, calling out the name of the little girl. Remembering what I thought was a dream, I went around the corner and continued to call out the little girl's name. After about an hour of searching, we made a 911 call to report that the little girl was missing.

Wishing that I had kept the little girl the night before, or that I could have reacted to what I saw as I slept, my heart sunk, as we waited to hear if someone had found the little girl. Finally, someone came to the phone to let us know that a man brought the little girl down to the police station, but a responsible adult, who would foster the little girl, would have to pick the child up. Luckily, one of Regina's aunts took the job of fostering, and it was a while before the little girl could come back home.

A friend loves at all times, and a brother is born for adversity. Proverbs 17:17

A Bone- Chilling Experience

I didn't drive as a teen. I didn't have a car, so I found no need for a driver's license. At 23 and married, I was still unlicensed, but we had a car that sat in our driveway for lack of a driver. My husband was deployed, and unless I was more confident at driving and was licensed, the car would sit for an additional five months. A friend, Wilhelmina, took me driving until I was confident enough to get a license. It was a relief to take the car back and forth to work.

The car we owned was a Chevrolet Vega, purchased for $600.00 from another military officer. The apartment we lived in was our second apartment. The first was an apartment my husband found, while I was working on a Saturday night, at the department store. We had been married two days and didn't have our own place to live. Despite my asking him not to find an apartment in Ocean View, that was exactly where he found a furnished apartment for us to live. We moved in the same Saturday night, bringing with us sheets, towels, dishes, pots, pans, and our clothing. Coming to the apartment, we were stopped by a man who was helper to the manager, who didn't remember his deal with my husband, that my husband could stay for the weekend with just paying the deposit, which he had paid. On the following Monday he would pay that month's rent, when the bank was open, and he could retrieve the money.

We went in for my tour of the apartment, and to live in our new home. As we settled in for the night, as we were in bed, the sound of a key in the lock startled us. The night latch stopped the entrance of the intruder. I got the eeriest feeling that this was not the place to live. My husband would get up at 5:00 a.m. to go to his ship on base, and I would be left alone. I let him know that I didn't feel good about staying here. He assured me it would be alright. I would just have to get more familiar with living here.

About 8:00 a.m., there was a very loud banging at our door. It was two police officers. They wondered why we were living in the apartment without permission. They asked us to get dressed and meet them directly downstairs, at the landlord's apartment. We quickly complied.

At the landlord's door, slightly opened, we noticed a thin, frail man sitting on his bed. After a brief conversation we found he was just out of the hospital. The subject of this meeting was the helper we had met outside, the night before. He had allegedly, broken into several apartments, on Saturday night, stealing money, television, stereos, jewelry and whatever else of value, he could find, along with our deposit, and took off. The helper had given my husband a receipt, scribbled on a torn corner of paper, and signed. The manager recognized the helper's handwriting. My husband also told the landlord that he was promised that he could pay the rent on Monday, which was the next day, and the landlord agreed. With the police officers satisfied with what we told them, we returned upstairs. I told my husband that I didn't plan to stay there another day. I asked my mother if we could stay at her house until my husband was back from his next deployment, which would be in September of the following year, and we moved back out of the apartment.

Back at my parent's house, my husband kept his routine, leaving 5:00 a.m. to get to muster on time, and I continued my job at the department store. It was business as usual, until I picked up a newspaper that Wednesday. The headlines read something like, "Landlord found beaten to death was left behind the door left ajar, at his apartment." I was so relieved that we decided to leave when we did. I can't imagine how I would have reacted if I were on my way to work in the morning and had passed the open door of the deceased, with his body exposed. I got chills just thinking about it. I was no longer anxious to live on my own.

Those who forsake the law praise the wicked, but such as keep the law contend with them. Proverbs 28:4

What About the Children?

When I was a child, there were two women from St. Paul C.M.E. Church who influenced my life so very much. It was through their kindness that, though my mom couldn't afford it, I had the opportunity to attend the kindergarten at the church. They went out of their way for my safety. They would either pick me up or wait for me to come out of my house, then help me across Virginia Beach Boulevard, safely. They would make sure that I would never attempt to cross alone. In the church, it was these ladies who looked for many opportunities for me to recite, although, being very shy, I declined many times, as well. When my oldest sister Carolyn sang a solo, it was usually because Mrs. Archer had already picked a song out. Or, at times, Mrs. Archer wanted both Loretta and Carolyn to sing together. Carolyn sang soprano and Loretta sang alto; together they sang beautifully. It was much later in life that Mrs. Archer and her sister Miss Gullens, asked me to sing with them. I only remember my sisters and I singing together once. We sang the song, *How Great Thou Art.* Carolyn sang soprano, Loretta sang alto, and I sang mezzo-soprano. When we sang unexpectedly for the church that day, one elderly man said we sounded like we were singing with the angels. While we practiced, just before we went out before the church to sing, that was my prayer.

Later, I joined the adult choir and got to sing with my sisters in the choir. We would go to weekly choir rehearsals, and somehow the sound of the choir added to the warm feeling of attending church on Sundays.

When my oldest daughter was almost two years old, we had come home from a friend's father's funeral, and I left my children in the living room to play, while I sat in my bedroom to work on some songs I was developing. For whatever reason, my little daughter came to me crying. She couldn't explain to me why she was so sad, but her tears inspired the song I would write about her brother and her, and in honor of Mrs. Archer and Miss Gullens, her sister:

Tears streaming down, her heart is broken

And because her life is hurting, so am I;

He wears a frown, his dreams are choking,

And because he stands alone his dreams could die.

So humbly I come to You, upset —
As I sound aloud the roof fell out today;
Hear me I pray.
What about the children? To ignore them is so easy;
So many innocent children, who choose their own way —
Yes, what about the children? Remember when we were children,
And if not for those who loved us, and who cared enough to show us,
Where would we be today?

So where is your son, where lies his refuge?
If he can't come to you, where can he run?
Such a foolish girl, yet still she's your daughter,
And if you will just reminisce, your days are young
You see it's not where you've been or what you've done —
Because I know a friend who specializes in great outcomes;
His love overcomes.
And what about the children? To ignore them is so easy;
So many innocent children, who choose their own way —
Yes, what about the children?
Remember when we were children,
And if not for those who loved us,
And who cared enough to show us,
Where would we be today? Where would we be today?
What about children?
Don't just turn and walk away —
What about children? They need our love and help today —
What about the children? Remember when we were children;
And if not for those who loved us, and who cared enough to show us,
Where would we be today?
What about the children?

This was written about my son and my daughter, but also in memory of
two sisters, Mrs. Mary Archer and Miss Gullens, who through their great love
for children turned many lives around.

Behold, children are a heritage from the Lord, the fruit of the womb is a reward. Like arrows in the hand of a warrior, so are the children of one's youth. Happy is the man who has his quiver full of them; They shall not be ashamed, but shall speak with their enemies in the gate. Psalm 127:3-5

A Struggle to Survive

Life was challenging enough, but mother nature has its fiery at times. I was finishing up my last semester at Norfolk State College and school was out for the summer. I had left a sketch pad and some painting supplies in the art room. I knew that if I didn't retrieve them, someone else might take them home to use them. It was so hot, I wore light pastel colors to reflect sunlight and stay cool. My light beige pants, and white blouse with a pastel print was the coolest outfit I had for this day. I talked to the art office manager, a young lady I had become friends with, and after she had lunch, I went out to take my first of two buses back home.

Waiting for the first bus, the sun was very hot as it shone down on my neck, and in my face. I cupped my hands over my eyes several times to block the sun, but after a few minutes, I got the bus and headed downtown. Downtown was no different, as the sun was equally as hot. I stood in front of a bus shelter and waited for the second bus, painting supplies in my hand. A few minutes in the wait, I looked towards the waterfront and there was a low cloud forming over the water. At second glance, I knew a tornado was forming over the water.

I went directly across the street to the Lerner Shops for shelter, but as I reached the door, the lady standing on the other side of it, was locking it. I looked towards other stores, only to find managers were locking their doors as well. They must have known something I did not know. I had no choice but to take shelter at the bus shelter. When I went back across the street to the bus shelter, behind the bench, the safest place, there was a young middle-aged black guy already standing in the back of the bench in the farthest corner, for safety. I joined him, but when an elderly, white lady joined us, I asked if she wanted to stand between me and the man, for her safety, and she agreed, so we switched places, leaving me on the outermost part of the inside of the shelter, still behind the bench. The beautiful, sunny day immediately turned to darkness, as dark storm clouds filled the sky. I checked to see the status of the tornado, and it was rotating and seemed to be moving. In my mind, I braced for the worst.

As this tornado began to move towards us, torrential rain began to pour. Lightening flashed so close to our faces, I thought I would be struck at every flash. Soot began to fly, letting us know that the tornado was getting closer.

As it drew near, I saw one brave lady who didn't want to stand at the shelter, feeling she could make it home, walk off a ways, then rose in the air like a balloon, but then I turned my attention back to the tornado heading towards us. A large cloud of soot raced towards us, rain continued to beat against us, such that we could feel its sting. We began to gasp for breath, as all of the oxygen seemed to be sucked upward. We gripped the bench in front of us for dear life, as we listened to the rhythmic sounds of the shelter, as it bumped up and down, the tornado trying to snatch it right out of the ground. I kept checking to see how much of the bolt was out of the ground, because, if we lost the shelter, we might be lost, as well. We constantly gasped for breath, as the tornado was beginning to pass over head. At one point, it seems like I wouldn't make it for lack of air, so I checked to make sure that the elderly woman was still breathing, and still holding on. I prayed like never before. Soon we were in its eye and we could breathe easier, what a relief, but the rain still poured and the lightning still flashed. Soon, as the tornado continued to move, the gasping started again as we again fought for air. The tornado continued to move, until soon it was gone. The sun came back out bright and hot, as if the tornado had never come. The devastation behind us was quite evident that there had been a tornado, with lamps, from poles behind us down, shattering windows of some of the cars in the parking lot, behind the shelter. But as I looked at each of the three of us at the shelter, we had survived. As I finally saw my bus coming, I got on the bus, standing near its entrance, drenched with rain, sooty from the ashes of the tornado, and not wanting to talk about it. As I reached my stop and got off of the bus, the danger was still not over. As I reached the walkway of the street leading home, live wires in the standing water hissed at me as I jumped across them to avoid electrocution. This was a trying day. I finally reached home.

When I knocked, my mother answered the door talking about the tornado, but as she looked at me, she knew I was in it. She insisted, "Hurry and get out of those clothes, and soak them so that the soot would come out!" I bathed and changed into dry clothes and before I knew it, it was time to go to work. I guess there is no rest for the weary.

But He said to them, "why are you so fearful, O you of little faith?" Then He arose and rebuked the winds and the sea, and there was a great calm. Matthew 8:26

A Misled Child

The scariest thing about raising a child, is to have the child influenced by others. The parent pours his love into a child and expects that child to be obedient. I still believe in spanking a child for disobedience, when some parents might give a child a time out. The fact is, some children will listen to reason and doesn't require a lot of spankings, and others, as my dad would put it, "are hard headed." I don't believe in using the "naughty chair" approach, because it is not the chair that's naughty.

Once, my oldest child, my son, got into trouble at home when he was about six years old. I told him he was going to get a spanking. He reached for the telephone, so I asked him who he was going to call. He said, "My teacher told me if my parents spanked me, I could call 911." I told him if he ever called 911 because I spanked him, I would give him a good reason to dial.

When he was a little older, one evening, he did not arrive from school on time. At 4:00 p.m. he was not at home, 4:30 p.m., not 5:00, nor even at 6:00. I worried so much that something had happened to him. I called his friends to see if he was at their houses, but he was not there. I asked the neighbors if they had seen him, but they had not. Tears filled my eyes, as I frantically searched for him, constantly listening for the phone to ring. At around 6:30, he came through the door. I asked him where he had been. He told me that he was playing video games with a middle schooler he had met at school. He said the little boy's father said he could stay with the little boy until he returned from work. These kids are the same age, I thought, why is my son, of the same age, going to babysit this man's son until he returns from work, and without my knowledge nor permission? I told my son that every day, I expected him to come directly home from school. He was not to stop to play video games with anyone, and because he had no permission and did not ask for permission, nor give me a call to ask if he could stay so late, he was going to get spanked, something I rarely did, because he didn't do things to get into trouble.

After talking about how this man would have never allowed his son to do what he had asked my son to do, and because my son knew I wouldn't allow it anyway, I spanked him, probably more than I should have, out of anger and all of the worry he had put me through. After the spanking, my son looked at me as if he were deeply hurt. He looked as if the belt I used had cut through him. He didn't cry, but I felt his hurt. He felt that he was helping that family, but in doing so, he had hurt me deeply.

I never spanked him again, but he never gave me a reason to. He always listened to my instruction before, until he let another parent tell him it was alright to do what he knew I wouldn't allow.

A violent man entices his neighbor, and leads him in a way that is not good. Proverbs 16:29

Fresh Flowers

Loretta was not only my sister, as time went on, she was my best friend. Through the years, we learned to lean on each other for support, and for strength. We had many hours conversing, talking for hours about our spouses, our children, church, and a loving God who had and continually helps us to keep it together. Lately, Loretta had been in and out of the hospital due to cancer. On a Sunday after church, I decided to visit her. De Paul Hospital was a lot closer than visiting her at her house in Suffolk, Virginia. This was a bright, warm sunny day, and I had planned to make the most of it.

Entering the hospital room, all I could see was pitch blackness. My eyes searched the dark room, to find Loretta, but I saw no one. I was beginning to think that I was in the wrong room. I called out, "Loretta, are you here?" And she answered, "I'm here, over by the window." I said, "Good afternoon, I came to spend a little time with you. How are you today?" Well, before she could answer, my son, Joshua, started wallowing in my arms, and couldn't be comforted, no matter how hard I tried. I asked where her bathroom was, and if I could go in there to pray. Upon entering the restroom, I prayed. The room was so dark, I sensed a demonic presence, so I prayed, and rebuked the devil off of my child, off of my sister, and off of that room. At the end of my prayer, giving thanks for God's mercies, I stepped back into Loretta's room.

The room was bright. The blinds were closed, but the bright sunshine came beaming through the window, as it had beamed when I was outside of the building, and I could finally see Loretta, and everything in the room. I could finally see the location of the chair I had eased into when I first entered the room. We began another conversation, and laughed and joked with each other as we had in the past. As we talked, a priest stuck his head in the door. He looked around a bit, then said that the room smelled like fresh flowers. Loretta then said, "When the Holy Ghost is present, it is said that the room smells like fresh flowers." She made a believer out of me, because there was not one flower in the room. We talked for a while, then I had to go home to take care of my other children.

Our family, like many others, had gone through many trials. It seemed like, if it weren't one thing, it was another. Loretta was out, then back in the hospital. Life had given me many lemons, but I was learning to "make lemonade." But most of all, when the situation was beyond my personal strength, I knew to call on God. I finally figured it out. This battle was not mine; this battle belonged to the Lord. I couldn't fight it. One day I was told in the spirit, "Behold, I give you power to tread over serpents and scorpions, and over all the power of the enemy, and nothing shall by any means hurt you." The word of God says, "Nevertheless do not rejoice in this, that the spirits are subject to you, but rather rejoice because your names are written in heaven." Now that's an "Allelujah!"

The next hospital stay for Loretta was at Norfolk Sentara Hospital. As soon as I would think things were getting much better, it seemed we were right back to square one. When I visited her, we talked mainly about scripture for the Lord was my strength, and I wanted her to lean on Him. I wanted her eyes to be truly opened to His word, as they were in the past. It seemed that the illness was not only trying to rob her of life, but it seemed to also be robbing her of her faith. At these times I would hear the Lord say, "The word is near you, even in your mouth, and in your heart; that is the word of faith, which we preach. If you confess with your mouth the Lord Jesus, and believe in your heart that God has raised Him from the dead, you shall be saved. For with the heart man believes unto righteousness, and with the mouth, confession is made unto salvation."

These words encouraged both of us. We shared many words of encouragement, until I realized that time had passed such that, if I didn't leave immediately for the bus home, I would have to wait an hour, in the dark, for the next bus. I prayed with Loretta, and let her know that, because of the bus schedule, and I had visited alone this particular night, it was time for me to leave. I had prayed that the angels would watch over her and keep her safe. As I rushed down the hall, to reach the waiting bus, I heard Loretta calling me. I rushed back to hear what she needed. She told me that in my hurry to leave, I didn't close out my prayer. My eyes were open to the scene in the room. It seemed like a dozen angels were in the room. The angels, dressed in long white robes, were over the bed, beside the bed on either side, and at least one of the angels was at the foot of the bed. The minute I said, "Amen," the angels were gone. I know that there would be no way she could have slept having so many angels all over the place, but when I think back now, they seemed to have provided a sense of peace.

Soon, Loretta was out of the hospital again. We constantly communicated by phone, since I didn't always have transportation to her house. She would say, "Beverly, as long as you're around, I feel strong, and the minute you are not here, I feel tired and sick again." I knew that it wasn't me, but the Lord, who was our strength.

When I was in labor to have my fifth child, Joseph, Loretta came from Suffolk to Norfolk, to take me to the hospital. That was a 35-minute drive, but not only did she come to pick me up, she went 20 minutes out of the way to pick up our mom, to babysit my other children. If that were not enough, knowing it was already 10:00 p.m. and my kids hadn't had dinner, she bought Long John Silver's sea food for all in my house to eat. Despite all she had gone through, and was still going through, she went out of her way for my family. My husband had spent his day and night out, and had no way of knowing I was in labor. Thank God for a sister, who cared enough to help, and for God giving her the strength. When I searched my mind for someone to help that day, because of her battle with cancer, I didn't want to ask her for help, but I was running out of options, since my husband was not picking up his phone.

I got to the hospital in the nick of time. At home, I served all of the children and my mother, and cleared the table, then made sure I had everything I needed for my hospital stay. By the time we reached the hospital and I was put in a wheel chair, it was midnight. Well, 15 minutes later, Joseph was born. I had asked Loretta not to wait for the birth; she still had a 35 minute trip back to Suffolk, and it was the next afternoon that she learned she had another nephew, and his length and weight.

We spent the next two years conversing at least three or four days out of a week, and we always talked about scripture. I believed that God would take the cancer away from her, if she would just believe that He would. I constantly prayed about it, hoping we would be around for each other for a long time. My husband lost his brother, and my family had planned to go to Philadelphia for the funeral. Since Loretta and I were in constant touch with each other, I told her of our plans and how long I would be gone. She said, "I don't want you to go. If you leave I feel that I won't be here when you get back." I told her that I had to go, being that he was my brother-in-law, but I would come to see her as soon as we got back. The stay at my mother-in-law's house in Philadelphia was three days, and I constantly prayed for Loretta, remembering what she had said. I believed that she would be fine, no matter where I was.

The day I got back to Norfolk, I went to see my sister. She was not fine. All she could do was sleep, though I kept talking to her and assuring her I was there. That was the last opportunity I got to see her alive. After her funeral, I wrote this song:

I remember the first time she laughed with me.

I remember the promises, she would never leave my side,

Now I'm standing with this news of a tragedy, standing with a fragile heart.

You see I never shed a tear, I stayed strong for them —

When everybody disappeared, (Lord) it was only You to keep me strong and I

Can't imagine going on, without her in my life,

But I'm going on with a fragile heart.

When I think about, think about life, Lord I think of You

I can't think of anything else, there's only You and I —

I can't think about ever giving up, can't give up;

The only thing that matters Lord is You!

But while I got some time to take, (sis) I'm missing you

I know you'd been in pain, and if it had not been for all the hurt inside

I would have cherished every moment we spent,

As a gift from God above, for He takes care of all fragile hearts.

When I think about, think about life, Lord I think of You;

I forget about everything else, there's only You and I —

I can't think about ever giving up, can't give up;

The only thing that matters, when I'm going through

Is giving that fragile heart right back to You.

When I lost my sister, my mind went back to the first time I remembered of one of many times we had a good belly laugh together. We were in the local library, and she needed books for a class assignment. She left me at a table reading books, as she searched many shelves for books she needed. It was probably only about 30 minutes she had left me, but to me it was hours, as my eyes searched for the sister I couldn't find. Because she told me to stay at the table, where she had left me, I was afraid to move. Afraid she wouldn't find me if I searched for her in that big library, I began to cry. She shortly came back with an arm full of books and asked if I were alright. I told her I was afraid she had left me. She said, "I would never leave you," and we both began to laugh. I was just seven years old at the time, and she was a fifteen-year- old. After that day, we had many opportunities to laugh together, share our silly jokes, and talk about funny things that happened in our families. I would never cry in front of my children if I could help it, but when my children left the room after I found out my sister had died, the tears poured, as I had lost a sister and a best friend that I would deeply miss.

God is our refuge and strength, a very present help in trouble. Therefore we will not fear, even though the earth be removed, and though the mountains be carried into the midst of the sea; Though its waters roar and be troubled, though the mountains shake with its swelling. Psalm 46:1-3

When I am a little sad and lonely, I remember the goodness of the Lord. The scripture says, "There is a river whose streams shall make glad the city of God, the Holy place of the tabernacle of the Most High. God is in the midst of her, she shall not be moved;" (Psalm 46:4-5)

The scripture reminds me of a song I wrote, with a little Shakespeare in its wording:

The song is called "A Secret Place" about the refuge of God, the tabernacle we can run to, when life throws so many curve balls, we are soon out of the game. I had to remember in all of these things, we are more than conquerors through Him who loved us. Romans 8:37

Tithing

In the Bible, the Israelites were required to give one tenth of the first fruits, whether it be money or livestock or grain, to the Lord, recognizing Him as their creator. This was a way of giving back what He required of His people, the children of Israel. The money, meat, and grain were used to keep up the work in the Tabernacle, provided for the priests who worked in the temple, the Levites. But also, money was used to feed the poor, and to care for them.

In our family, my husband was a tither long before I was. He would give ten percent of his income for a tithe, and he would give offerings to the church. I was too stingy to give as I should. He would say he was giving enough to cover our household, which was great, because I would give whatever I felt like giving, that particular Sunday, at church. When I didn't go to church, I didn't give. I watched my husband not only give tithes and offerings at the local church, he would give large offerings and vows to television ministries.

When we lived in a two-bedroom apartment, and our refrigerator was leaking such that I would have to get the water up from the front of the refrigerator at least once or twice a day, for weeks. I begged my husband for a new refrigerator. We would argue for weeks, about the need for a new refrigerator. Finally, my husband told me, "If you want a new refrigerator, pray for one!" Now God surely had provided all of my needs, but I had never seen Him send down things like refrigerators before. At this time, Wayne was so wrapped up in his local church and their greed, outside of tithing he had neglected his own family. At my continual insistence, my husband finally purchased a new refrigerator, that lasted for at least ten years after we had moved it into our new home.

As an employee of the Norfolk Public School System, at some point, I learned how to tithe and give offerings based on my income. This had to be close to the year 1990. I had seen the way God had taken care of my family. I know that it was a very small thing to give back to Him a small portion of the many great things He had given to me. When I would sing, "He has done great things, bless His holy name," I meant it from the bottom of my heart. Someone said at church once, "You can't beat God's giving," and I know that to be true. There is no calculating the blessings of God. They are innumerable!

Will a man rob God? Yet you have robbed Me! But you say, "In what way have we robbed You? In tithes and offerings. You are cursed with a curse, for you have robbed Me, even this whole nation. Bring all of the tithes into the storehouse, that there may be food in My house, and try Me now in this, says the Lord of hosts, "If I will not open for you the windows of heaven and pour out for you such blessing that there will not be room enough to receive it."
Malachi 3:8-10

The Naming of Children

In naming the children, though our son was born first, my husband never wanted a son with his same name, so I made up a name that sounds like Wayne, my husband's name. This was my only child for six years. After he was born, the obstetrician said, due to complications from his birth, I would never have another child. He was born weighing eight pounds and fourteen ounces, and though he was born in December, his due date was actually sometime in February. There was a mix-up in the military records, that were transferred to Sentara Norfolk General, where my child was born. The military doctor thought I was not actually pregnant when I first visited his office, but I insisted, and returned to his office two other times, until he showed me in a book that I was having a hysterical pregnancy. He told me I wanted a baby so much, that I had convinced myself that I was pregnant. My body was showing all of the symptoms. I was as skinny as a rail; maybe he just couldn't tell.

I was convinced that he couldn't be right, so I visited the family planning clinic near the downtown section of Norfolk, and after a urine sample, the nurse told me I was a least a few months pregnant. Being that the military doctor I had visited was my designated doctor, I took the results back to him, and he said, "You must have just got pregnant." Well, with the urine test done again, confirming what I already knew, he started prenatal visits. That explains my large first child, born two months premature.

Even when the doctor had told me I would have no more children , I became pregnant, six years later, with a second child. I thought back to a day my father invited me to dinner at his house. Knowing my husband was usually at home from work by five, Dad asked me to come at about 4:00 p.m. I arrived on time, looking forward to the coleslaw and barbeque that he promised he would prepare. When I arrived, he said he had something to tell me, as I joined him in the living room. As I got ready to sit, there was a strange light on his face. I tried to block its path, but the light was still there. I didn't yet understand its source until he started speaking. He said he had been reading his Bible more, and he had just finished reading the "begots," referring to the book of Matthew. He told me, before I was expecting a second child, that I would have several other children, besides my child I had with me. He began to name the other children, Christina, Malcolm (who would say aupple instead of apple), Joshua, Joseph, and Esther. My dad also said that he only had about six months to live, and he would never see the other children. At this, we both sat and cried.

Thinking back on what the doctor had said, feeling I would never have another child, my mind wandered to another place. To further convince me that this was from God, he told me that although my son was hungry and had not yet had lunch, he would feed my husband first. Dad said, "Though he was hungry, my son would not eat from my husband's plate, but as soon as he served me, my son would eat off of my plate."

My husband joined us around 5:30 p.m. My dad promptly gave him a plate of food. He ate it, as our son played near him, not interested in what he was eating. Then my dad prepared my plate, and gave it to me. My son rushed over to the plate, grabbed a handful of barbeque, and stuffed his mouth. Truly what he had told me comes from the Lord.

Well, I was expecting a second child and things at home were, to say the least, complicated. My husband had expressed his interest in becoming a Mason, and for whatever reason, stayed out of the house two and three nights at a time. I knew I was having a second child, but he wasn't aware of this yet. After a few more weeks, with his continuously staying away from home, I told him that we were expecting a second child. He said, "I don't mind taking care of one child, but I'm not going to take care of two." When things continued pretty much the same, I asked him to get his clothes and leave. I didn't think about the fact that I had no job, and I would soon have two children to take care of. The next few weeks after my husband had left were a struggle. The first of the month was coming and bills would be due, including the rent, and the food was low. I had no choice but to ask for support through the court system, to assure that we would have regular income in the house. We rationed food, and soon the court date came and I thought the pressure of having very little money would ease up. When the judge only awarded enough to pay the rent, even after I told him we were expecting another child, I was floored. I didn't think, with my husband's income, the judge could be so insensitive.

I cried about it when I returned home, then I had a vision: I was looking at the curb in front of the apartment that we lived. On it was a large heap of furniture and household items. Then the Lord spoke, "This won't be you; Your husband will pay your bills, and after a year, he will return home. Do those things that you should do." I was relieved that we could stay in our apartment. It was now 1984. My father died April 1, 1981. He would never see my second child. Months went by and my daughter was born. I had no name in mind for her, as I had forgotten my dad's prophecy. My son asked if we could name her after his two girlfriends from second grade. We did. We named her Christina Michele, and he loved her dearly. I liked the name Christina because, when the "a" is placed on the other side of the "n," you have the word Christian, something I wanted all of my children to become. My husband would visit every now and then, and didn't express a lot of interest in the new baby. On the first of each month, he paid the bills, bought food, and bought a few clothes for the kids. I used the money from the support to pay rent, such that if it were late because of the mail, my landlord told me to pay it in halves, one half the first of the month and the other in the middle of the month. I didn't see how that would work, but it did. For a year, the bills were paid and we rationed food, but the financial stability was not there. I thought about what the Lord had promised; "For all the promises of God in Him are Yes, and in Him Amen, to the glory of God through us." (2 Corinthians 1:20) I reminded the Lord that he said my husband would be back home in a year.

Two weeks later, there was a knock on the door. I opened the door to see my husband. He explained how he had been living out of his car for the past two weeks, and still having to go to work, he was just tired. I told him to put his clothes from the car away and rest.

My third child was conceived, two years after my husband returned home. Things still weren't the way they should be. A lot of distrust was there and attendance to church seemed to be the only thing we did as a family. Knowing how rocky the marriage was, I did not discuss the fact that another child was coming. As I sat in a chair in the living room crying, from about 8:00 a.m. until noon, my two-year-old walked over to me. She said, "Momma, don't cry, don't you know that children are a gift from God. Now get up and get me something to eat!" Well, I knew where that was coming from. I got up and prepared a late breakfast, a brunch. I later told my husband about the new little one coming. He said like he took care of the two we had, he would take care of this child.

When the child was born, my husband thought he would name this child after his grandfather. Since he couldn't remember his grandfather's name, he named this child Malcolm. I tried to tell him that wasn't his grandfather's name, but he said, "Somehow I think we should stick to that name." Wayne's grandfather was called Mark. It was many years later that we found out his name was actually Nicklaus, as we searched ancestry.com. When Malcolm learned to talk and he would ask for an apple, calling it an aupple, it jogged my memory to the conversation with my father. I still couldn't remember all my dad had told me.

Three years later, we went from a store front church of about ten members, to a larger church with a couple thousand members, such that, there were two church services, one at 8:00 a.m., and the other at 11:00 a.m. My family usually attended the earliest service. At times I would attend intercessory prayer with my husband. We studied the Bible more, though sometimes we argued about that, as my husband would try to interpret meanings of various scriptures. As Wayne sat in the church one day, he heard from God. God told him that he would have another child, and his name would be Joshua. I had only known a few months that I was expecting a child, but I was ignoring the symptoms, because we had been living in a two-bedroom apartment with three children already, the house was getting a little crowded. Wayne anxiously told me what the Lord had told him, so I shared what I knew. Joshua, a very bubbly child, who hardly ever cried, was born three years after Malcolm. The thing that caused Joshua discomfort and tears was whenever he was in demonic presence.

Still another time, only a year after Joshua was born, Wayne was sitting in the church when the Lord spoke to him again, letting him know that he was having another child. That child was to be called Joseph. Here I was, pregnant again. By now, I was wondering why I was having child after child, after child. I thought about the doctor, telling me I wouldn't have another child after the first child. Now I would have a fifth child, and instead of complaining, I remembered my daughter telling me when she was a toddler that children are a gift from God. Boy, was I getting a lot of gifts. By the time Joseph was a young teen, he had many dreams that he would talk about.

A year later, Wayne came home from church again, telling me that God told him that, yet again, we would have another child, a little girl named Esther. I seemed to have a baby every other year at this time, but I got excited that I was finally having another girl. My girls would be eleven years apart in age, but it was exciting to have another girl in the house. The unusual thing about Esther is that she would use big words all the time. At six years old, when I had to ask my children to write something about me in an autobiography I was writing for school for my advanced English class, she wanted to write something as well. I was intrigued when she wrote what a marvelous mother she had because I bought everything she wanted. Then she listed the things: hamburgers, candy, and toys. I think Esther was born "for such a time as this." I thank God for the children. I love each one of them.

Well, with my last three children born every year and a half, I seriously thought about celibacy. One morning, not knowing whether to use birth control or not, with God blessing us with children, in my bathroom mirror as I washed my face, I prayed to the Lord that I wouldn't give birth to another child. Immediately, the gentle voice of a female angel spoke to me. She said, "Don't pray that. You are asking for a curse. The Lord has closed the wombs of the women who can't have children." I repented that I had prayed the prayer. Later, having a husband and six children, and living in a two-bedroom apartment, I asked God to please find us a place to live, that my children had their own rooms. My oldest son, Lewayne, was a teenager, and definitely needed his own space. Weeks later, I got off of the wrong bus to get home, and got off at the wrong stop. As I walked through the neighborhood, the Lord directed my eyes to a large sign stuck in the grass. I read it, and it told of a special program for people who grew up in or had lived for some time in the area. I wrote down the number, called, and representatives of the organization sent people to our house to explain the program. We went to meetings, signed contracts, and our house was built in a little over a year. A few years after the house was built, I became a substitute teacher. I financed a new van for our family. The new house had four bedrooms, two and a half baths, and a loft, an open area for the laundry and for the children to play. It seemed like overnight things were looking up.

It is the Lord's mercies that we are not consumed, because his compassions fail not. They are new every morning: great is thy faithfulness. The Lord is my portion, saith my soul, therefore will I hope in him. The Lord is good unto them that wait for him, to the soul that seeketh him. Lamentations 3:22-25

Anointed Prophetess

At the store front church, my husband had spent many Sundays preaching . We were expecting a prophetess from New Jersey to visit this church. I had never visited a church in the presence of a prophet or a prophetess before. I wondered what she would say, or do. My husband had been elevated in the ministry, from deacon, to co-pastor. He had attended the local branch of Virginia Union University, and he and I together read books and scriptures, then compared notes. It was at these times God seemed so close, and I would write several songs about my many Christian experiences. At this time, Joseph was only about two weeks old, and all of the other children had gone ahead to church with their dad. As I stood at the sink washing dishes from the night before, the Lord spoke, saying, "Put $20.00 in church today." I separated the money from the other money I had after washing the dishes, and dressed myself and my son for church.

Stepping through the door of the church, the prophetess looked into my eyes, as I looked at her. I knew she was the prophetess we were expecting, because she was the only person there I didn't recognize. I had also invited my sister Carolyn to the church, and she brought my mother along. I looked for where they were seated, then took a seat beside them. After a few devotional songs, the prophetess was introduced, then came up to speak. The first thing she asked was that as many people who could bring $20.00 up to put in the basket, where she had been standing. I put my money in the basket, then went back to my seat. She called people up, who wanted prayer. She prayed for several people, laying hands on some of them, then looked at me as I was still seated. She asked me to come up. Standing before her, my husband holding the baby near an area where he was sitting, Prophetess Hall began to talk about how God had been dealing with her, concerning me, the minute I came through the door. She had me sing, *I love You Lord Today* , as she prepared some oil. She told me the Lord wanted her to anoint me a prophetess. She reminded me of the Lord's calling me when I was seven years old . That particular day, I was leaving my cousin Deborah's house, because she couldn't come out to play. As I walked back home, what looked like a ball of fire a few feet off the ground, was behind me. As I looked back for the person calling Deborah, I saw the flames of fire, in a ball. Prophetess Hall told me that God was calling me, even then. She told me of all the times the Lord had been in-strumental in my life. And with my singing the song over and over, tears streaming down my face, pouring oil upon my head, I was anointed, prophe-tess, in the name of Deborah, one of the judges of Israel.

Surely the Lord God does nothing, unless He reveals His secret to His servants the prophets. A lion has roared! Who will not fear? The Lord God has spoken! Who can but prophesy? Amos 3:7-8

Better Never, Than Late

One morning, when Lewayne, my oldest son, was late for school, I got out of the chair I had slept in, from about 5:00 a.m. until 8:00 a.m., when he woke me up. He was dressed for school, but said that he thought he had missed the bus. Looking at the clock, he was right. Still a little tired from my postal clerk job, working on the third shift, I stood in the mirror to wash my face when a voice spoke to me. He said, "Don't take the car out today." I thought about it being a warm April 1ˢᵗ, after such a cold winter and thought I'd come right back home, and go nowhere else. Then the voice said, "You will break your neck." So I prayed that God would keep me safe, as I go to take Lewayne to school.

I had purchased a Fiat for $600.00 and couldn't locate the back seat belts. I put Christina in the front seat in her car seat, then let Lewayne sit in the back, with no seatbelts to secure him. We lived on 26ᵗʰ street at the time. I pulled out of the driveway, turned left onto the adjacent street, then turned left again onto 27ᵗʰ street, heading towards Colonial Avenue. As I approached Colonial, the traffic light was yellow so I came to a stop. Stopped, Lewayne asked why we had to stop for traffic lights anyway. I explained how traffic lights keep us safe. The light changed from red to green. I checked to make sure the traffic to my right and left had stopped, then proceeded across the intersection. As I reached the center of the intersection, in my peripheral vision, I saw a fast-moving oncoming car so close, I was about to be hit. I pressed the accelerator, such that the oncoming car would pass me from behind, and I could get across safely. Just when I thought we were safe, I heard the sound of several glass buildings crashing down around me. The jolt jack-knifed me from my seat to a metal part of the car above my head. I was about to pass out, but before I did, I heard Lewayne sliding from one side of the backseat of the car to the other, as the car went into a spin. As we were about to hit a pole on the street corner, I turned the wheel a bit, and a large spirit, the Holy Ghost, sat in the car behind the wheel, in the driver's seat. He stirred the car as it went into a violent spin. I had slumped into a deep sleep. Later, an officer woke me up to get the kids out of the car, because of an oil leak. He said it was urgent to hurry out of the car; the car could catch fire. The car was now midway in the block, facing the one-way traffic on 27ᵗʰ street.

I got out of the car, then walked with my two kids down the street to the officers standing near two police cars. I showed my license upon a police officer's request, but he put it in his pocket. I got the other person's information. The officer asked if we were alright, so I asked the kids how they felt. Other than a few scratches on Lewayne, from sliding back and forth in the car, we all seemed to be alright. As I started the trip back home , I passed the Boy's Club, then realized I had no clue where I lived. I was seeing vast sky and clouds, then seeing what was on earth again. Having two children with me, I didn't want them to worry, so I walked back to the officers, who were still standing and talking. I asked the officer holding my license, if I could have my license back. He asked, "What brought you back?" I said, "I can't remember where I live." He said, "Oh! I need to call an ambulance," and he did, but also had the car towed.

At DePaul hospital, I was told to call my husband so that he could watch the children, after they had been examined. I could only remember the phone number to the place where Wayne worked, when he first started working at the Naval Base, and that was five years ago. The new number, although I had used it several times, I could not remember. So happens that, the man on the base answering the phone, knew my husband and the work area he was transferred to. I reached my husband, explained we had been in an accident, and he rushed to the hospital. With Wayne taking care of the children, I was examined by the doctor. He noticed that my neck leaned over to the right. Upon further examination, he told me that my neck was broken, and if it had been injured any more, I would have died. He cupped both hands around my neck, and began fitting it back into its socket. I listened to the sound of cracking, as he twisted the bone back and forth until it completely fit into place. I didn't get a brace for my neck. The doctor said it would be helpful if I would use my neck in a normal fashion, I would think to keep it from stiffening. I returned home and other than minor aches, I felt alright.

Around midnight, everything in my body ached. Even my fingers ached, to the point where I didn't want to lie against anything. The kids complained of pain as well. I know it is the Lord who saved me. He even sent the Holy Ghost to guide the car. God is always faithful, even when I am disobedient. I know Lewayne would have been disappointed not going to school, but disappointment never hurt anyone.

You shall walk in all the ways which the Lord your God has commanded you, that you may live and that it may be well with you, and that you may prolong your days in the land which you shall possess. Deuteronomy 5:33

Airborne

I babysat my two nephews a whole summer one year. Seemed it was the hottest summer ever. At the time, my oldest son was sixteen, my daughter was ten, the middle child was seven, and the two youngest boys were four and two years old. Because boys could be so rambunctious, I sent my oldest son and my oldest nephew to the boys' club, and my other children and my five- year-old younger nephew stayed with me. At the club, the boys could swim, play basketball, play table games, and do many other activities. The place was well air conditioned, and great to be all day when it was as hot as this day was.

The older children being out, the younger children played in the house with the air conditioner on. Before I knew it, it was 11:30 a.m., and it was soon time for lunch. I asked the children what they would have for lunch, naming various sandwiches, but David, their cousin, wanted a tv dinner, so tv dinners it was. I prepared the children to go to the store, getting the stroller out for Joseph, my two-year-old, and headed out. We had to stop at the Colonial Boy's Club to find out the kind of dinners the other two boys would have. The Colonial Boy's Club was only three blocks down the street, but the walk seemed forever under the blistering sun. After two blocks, we crossed the street so that, at the end of the block, we would be directly across the street from the Boy's Club. With the sun blazing down on my neck, making sure Joseph was alright in the stroller, with the other boys close to me on either side of the stroller, and Christina walking along beside me, we finally reached the corner just across the street from the club.

Immediately, my eyes were drawn to an eighteen-wheeler crossing the intersection, heading for the far right lane, opposite the side we stood, and traveling down 26th street. Then came a dark green Jeep four by four trying to share the same lane, merging at the same time, such that their front wheels met. Feeling the impending danger, I looked back at the house and the grassy yard behind where we stood. I told the children to stand as far away from the corner as they could stand. I tried to move in that direction also, but my feet wouldn't move. They seemed to be plastered to the sidewalk. I pushed the stroller towards the other children, instructing them not to move, turning my belly away from the street, away from the direction of the truck. I was eight months pregnant with another child. When I looked back at the truck, the spikes on its front wheel had met the front wheel of the Jeep, and hurled the Jeep over two stories into the sky. Seeing this, my daughter came over to save me, but I told her to go back; I couldn't move. The Jeep moved at such an angle, when it reached its height, it was near the center of the intersection, then the Jeep leaned to the side, emptying its contents. The driver came out through the passenger side window and crashed into the ground with a splat, in the street just in front of my feet. With great fear in me, knowing the Jeep was also about to hit the ground, I thought, "Oh God, help!" Then the Jeep came crashing done in the street, right next to the man, but missing him. Christina asked if she could run to the phone just across the street, so I gave her two quarters for the 911 call. In her excitement and with all of her fear, disregarding oncoming traffic, she raced across the street to make the call.

The man, in pain and with much fear said, "Lady don't leave me out here by myself." I assured him I wasn't going anywhere. I told him that my daughter had called and an ambulance was on the way. The man's wallet had fallen out of his pocket, as he was thrown to the earth. The wallet landed a few feet from us. I saw a passerby when he picked it up and placed it in his pocket, and continued down Colonial Avenue. Hoping that the man was still coherent, he could give the medical staff his information, and as I stood with him, I could finally hear the sounds of sirens in the distance. Help was on the way. I told the man help was here, and I needed to get the kids out of the way, so the medical team could help him. We went across the street, to find out what the two boys in the club wanted for lunch, then continued to the store.

Back at home, after heating the dinners, the kids and I sat at the table talking about the day's event as we ate. My daughter had come to the conclusion that the tee shirt I was wearing was cursed. Thinking back, every time I wore the shirt, there was some kind of incident. It was big, and I wore it as a maternity blouse. With so little clothes to wear, and one month to go, I couldn't afford to let the blouse go.

The next few weeks I searched the newspaper for information on the accident. I wanted to know if the man had survived his ordeal, and to let him know what had happened to his wallet. I could never find the information, but with God's help, I'm sure he recovered.

For His anger is but for a moment, His favor is for life; Weeping may endure for a night, but joy comes in the morning. Psalm 30:5

An Unexpected Stop

Well, as the Fiat was totaled, I searched for another inexpensive call, to get me back and forth to my postal worker's job. I found a gold Renault Encore, and for only $700.00. I had found something I could afford. I prayed to the Lord that as I drove that car, that I would never hit a person, especially a child, and that I didn't cause any property damage either. I really wanted to say that I didn't want to get into another car accident!

I drove my Encore so much, for getting my children back and forth to school, for getting groceries, for visiting my mom, and for hauling laundry to the laundry mat to dry. It was also wonderful, not to have to run to a bus stop at 5:00 a.m. to get home to get the kids, so that my husband could leave for work. I would run, knowing the dangers of a young woman being out alone that early in the morning. I was relieved when I would find so many people at the bus stop waiting for their bus, most of them trying to get to work. Now that I had the Encore, life was so easy, leaving work, getting into the car in a parking lot well lit, and casually driving home. Much of the stress of having a third shift job, was leaving. At this time, I was still living on 26th street.

One kids-free afternoon, as I drove down a one-way street, cars parked closely on both sides of the street, my car came to a sudden, complete stop. As I sat, contemplating why the car had stopped, I looked around the area I was in, then saw a two-year-old. She came from between two of the parked cars, and ran right past the front of my car, to the other side of the street. Then I watched a young female, who had been casually standing with a screen door open, talking to someone. She rushed by my car, grabbed the little girl, then passed the front of my car again, to carry the little girl back to the porch. Again, God had saved me from a nightmare, I wouldn't want to have to live through. I continued to wherever I was going that day. I drove the Encore, until an engine problem a few years after my purchase made me give the car up.

How could you not want to be faithful, and serve a God who is always so very faithful? The word of God says, "If you are faithful over a few things, I will make you ruler over many."

His Lord said to him, "Well done, good and faithful servant; you have been faithful over a few things, I will make you ruler over many things. Enter into the joy of your lord." Matthew 25:23

Life With Mom

Mom had been truly a blessing throughout the years. In many events that called for a celebration, she was there. She told me when I was born, there was a strange light on my face. As a child, I didn't understand it. As I got older, I thought it might be one of the "old wives' tales." Actually, I never gave it a second thought, until I saw the strange light on my father's face when he began to prophesy about the children I would have.

When my youngest sons were ages two years old and eight months old, Mom had suffered a stroke. I would take a bus to see her with my sons on either hip as I walked from the bus stop to the nursing home, where she was in rehabilitation. She had to relearn to talk and to write again. The rehabilitation took about six months. Her walking also was a bit off balance, so she had to learn to walk correctly, as well. Out of the nursing home, other than medicine for diabetes, she was back on her feet. She felt pretty good most of the time, but at times she struggled with her health.

She visited me, staying overnight in our two- bedroom apartment. With Mom in the second bedroom, and the kids sleeping in other parts of the house, when she awoke the next day, she asked me to pray with her for healing. As I prayed, she held on to me, hugging me closely and rocking back and forth, and didn't let me go until the prayer was over. When my prayer ended, the Lord said, " Twenty-five years." Mom had wondered if she would die soon, because in 1981, Dad had died. She thought that she would soon follow him. It was near the end of 1993, and though she was sick from time to time, she was strong much of the time.

Mom was there at Esther's prekindergarten graduation, when I cried as Esther had reached that mile stone. With my six kids, my mom got to attend all their high school graduations. She was there to attend Christina's college graduation. On many occasions that were important to our family, Mom was there. In 2007, during the Virginia Tech massacre, I was at a school down the street from De Paul hospital, where she now was after a second stroke. As she had come through the first stroke, this time she had a very difficult time. Mom was thirty years older than I was, and recovery wasn't as easy now as it had been before.

Before 2007, Mom had spent a year in a nursing home different from the one she had been in before. She couldn't speak and she was fed through a feeding tube . She needed the kind of care this nursing home could offer. The care givers seemed caring, but sometimes she signaled her displeasure, as she couldn't talk now. When I visited her, not sure of what she was trying to tell me at times, I would make many statements, until I hit on the subject she was trying to talk about. She nodded yes or no, according to the answer she was trying to give. At one point, I gave her a notepad to write down what she was trying to say, but if she couldn't say it, she didn't want to express it in any other way. She spent a little over a year in the nursing home. Though she couldn't communicate through talking, we laughed together for many days. Then the nursing home called my oldest sister, who was in charge of her care, telling her that Mom had suffered another stroke. She was taken to Sentara Leigh Memorial Hospital for the care she needed. In a coma now, our family had to meet at the hospital, to decide how long she should stay on life support. That was a difficult decision ; taking her off meant letting her go. At the meeting, we had asked that she stay on life support a little longer, hoping she would pull through as she had before. The hospital didn't agree, with her running up a bill her insurance wouldn't cover. After the meeting, we found that she was already off life support, when we arrived at her room. Carolyn and I sat in my mother's room to spend more time with her. My brothers, James, Clayton, Rodney, and Steven, all went outside, for Rodney to take a cigarette smoking break. In Mom's room, there was a television on, showing beautiful mountain and ocean scenery from around the country. I sat in a chair facing the foot of her bed, beside Carolyn, as we talked about that day's events. As we sat talking, I noticed that Mom's eyes were open. I walked over to ask her how she was doing, and to let her know that I was there. She had a blank look on her face, coming out of a coma. I kissed her on her forehead twice and her spirit came out of her. I heard the Lord saying, "I told her that you would kiss her twice before she goes." A tear fell from my eye, as I watched her spirit waiting by the door. In my mind I told her, "It's alright , you can go. We will be alright." Simultaneously, her mouth opened, as she took her last breath, and the machines for her respiration started to alarm. Mom was gone.

Her homegoing was at St. Paul C.M.E., although it had been years since we had attended the church. That was the only church, other than the church her mom and siblings had attended, where Mom had membership . After the service and the cemetery trip, we went back to the church for food and fellowship, with church members we hadn't seen in years. Outside of the church, as my siblings and I stood in a semicircle, waiting to get in the family car to go back home, something from the sky above us came down and stood in the center. I said, "It must be Mom. She probably wants to make sure we take care of Steve (her youngest child)." At that, the presence departed, ascending as fast as it descended. We contemplated the presence for a moment, then got into the family car.

When I think back to the prayer and the day I had rocked with my mom, asking God for her healing through prayer, God had given her over twenty-five years from my dad's death until hers. Dad died April, 1981 and Mom died in August, 2007.

For we do not wrestle against flesh and blood, but against principalities, against powers, against rulers of the darkness of this age, against spiritual host of wickedness in the heavenly places. Ephesians 6:12

The Costume

Old Dominion University is where Christina attended, directly after high school. She had expressed wanting to become a student there, while she was attending a program for the past three summers, called Upward Bound. The director, Mrs. Toliver, seemed to favor her, as she was selected to be in many plays and other activities in the program. As we attended the plays and activities on a regular basis, our family seemed to have a sense of purpose. There was more to do now than just to work and come home to dinner, dishes, and television. The plays centered around social issues and the black church, as Christina and other students acted out various roles. Christina was a hardworking student, who even with two jobs kept good grades in school.

She also participated in ODU's other activities. One day she asked me to make a long dress for her, on a sewing machine she had purchased. She also purchased some baby blue shiny fabric, with lots of glitter, for constructing this dress. A pattern in her size was purchased to help complete the look of a dress that Cleopatra might have worn. With the little sewing skills I had, I put together the dress. When it was complete, it fit every curve Christina had. She loved it. While I was sewing the dress a song formed in my head, and I began to sing, thinking about life, and the things I had gone through. This is the song:

> Surely I've been through the storm and rain,
> I know everything about heartache and pain,
> But God has carried me through it all;
> Without His protection, I would surely fall.
> I've been broke without a dime to my name,
> but all my bills got paid because I called on Jesus name;
> You can't tell me that God isn't real,
> 'cause I've got the victory and that's why I'm still here.
>
> Chorus
> I got the victory, I got the sweet victory in Jesus, yes I do
> He's a mighty conqueror, if our minds would just halt, battles He'll fight;
> I got the victory, I got the sweet victory in Jesus

For me He died but He rose on the third day,
That's why I have true victory every day.

I'm not worried about material things I don't have
I just stand secure in my savior's care;
I know my blessings are on the way,
I can't see it right now, but I stand on faith.
I fought many, many battles in His name,
I've held up the blood-stained banner and proclaimed
That Jesus is the truth and the life;
Believe me when I tell you, He'll make it alright.

(chorus)

The song seemed to be the expression of the culmination of all of my struggles. I thought about the time when I had separated from my husband. A time when I didn't think I would financially make it. I thought of other times of shear heartache, my storms, and rain. Life was hard, but God had blessed me through it, every step of the way. Truly, without His protection, I could not stand.

Needless to say, my competitive daughter won in one of the categories, in the costume contest. Not only was Cleopatra a hit, her date, Mark Antony, was a hit as well.

For by grace you have been saved through faith, and that not of yourselves; it is the gift of God, not of works, lest anyone should boast. For we are His workmanship, created in Christ Jesus for good works, which God prepared beforehand that we should walk in them. Ephesians 2:8-10

Saved By Grace

No longer working for the postal service, again I was a stay-at-home mom. Previously, I was sorting flats as I worked on the workroom floor for the postal service one night. As machines whirled, making their rhythmic, loud, continuous, noises, and co-workers chattered about new songs or the latest fashions, I stood, in my own head, wondering what the day would bring. While sorting one pile of mail after the other, I saw something in the ceiling. It was a large check about five feet by eight feet in size. I became very excited. Would I win the lottery? Was I going to get a lot of money from an inheritance? My mind filled with explanations for the big check. Then the Lord's voice spoke, "You are just here for a big check. Your children need you at home. Leave this job and stay home with your children!" Thinking about what He said, I finished my work for the night, and thought about giving a two weeks notice to quit.

I reached home about 5:30 that morning, and the smell of smoke filled the air. I walked to the kitchen to see what was on fire. A pan was sitting on the stove that was half burned on the inside. I didn't know if it were salvageable. I looked up to black soot on what use to be a white ceiling over the stove. I wondered what had occurred while I was at work. I was about to talk to Lewayne for an explanation, but as I started out of the kitchen, Wayne walked in. He said he got up to make a snack because he was hungry. He went back to sleep, and slept, until my daughter Christina, a two-year-old, climbed over the rail of her crib, jerked his head up and down by the hair, and woke him up. Lewayne, still sleeping, had slept through the whole ordeal.

A year after our separation, Wayne had come home with a drinking habit he didn't have before he left. Every night, Wayne had to have a bottle of wine, that he emptied before he slept. This made him a bad candidate for watching the children, such that sometimes I would get my mother to come and babysit through the night. This had not been one of those nights. It was just Wayne and the children. I sat and thought about how dangerous this situation was. I knew why the Lord had showed me the big check. Not waiting until I went to work that night, I called my supervisor and told him I was not going to continue working there. This was around December 1986. I would miss the money not working, but I would not want to be without my children. It was at that time the Lord told me I was saved, as I wondered why He was always there to get me out of every terrible situation. I thought about how horrible it would have been if, while I worked, my family were trapped in a house fire, having only one door near the kitchen to exit. I wondered what kind of God spent so much time helping one person, me? I felt so unworthy. That was a feeling I continued to have, as He continued to show me, He is God! Thinking about all that God has done for me, I began to sing this original song:

I give all praises to You Lord
All that I am I owe it to thee;
Cleansed me from sin
Set my soul free, to share with others
What You've done for me.
Singing all because of You
Oh Lord it's all because of You;
Any good that I've done,
All that I do, is all because of You.
Because of the power, that's in Your name,
I can do all things, You strengthen me,
to be a witness, that the world might believe,
and give You glory in eternity.
Singing all because of You;
Oh Lord it's all because of You,
Any good that I've done; all that I do
is all because of You.
All because of You, I can
love all my neighbors as You said to do;
All because of You, I can stand against evil and say yes to You.
You give me strength, Yes You do;
I'll walk in Your ways;
You've been my shield from day to day, and it's
by Your grace, I'm saved because of You.
You're the reason why, I'm saved, because of You.
You're my love, my joy, my everything;
It's by Your grace I am saved; By Your grace I am saved,
Because of You!

Call to Me, and I will answer you, and show you great and mighty things, which you do not know. Jeremiah 33:3

A Scare at School

In 2007, I was a substitute teacher for the Norfolk Public School System. I had worked in this job for seven years now. My children were older now, and I had help collecting the children when they were out of school. My oldest son was between jobs at the time. My youngest child, a twelve-year-old, came home from school with her brothers, Joshua and Joseph, and Lewayne, their oldest brother, babysat until I was home from work. I enjoyed working with the many children I worked with, some of them I watched mature as I eventually would retire, working for the school system for 17 years.

As I kept my eyes on children playing on the playground, at Granby Elementary, a school that I substituted at frequently, I heard two teachers whispering to each other. I had substituted at this school so many times, the teachers knew that my oldest daughter, attended Virginia Tech for grad school. I had shared with them the activities of my children. When I was sure they didn't want me to hear what they were saying, yet looking towards me, one of the ladies saying, "She obviously doesn't know what's going on," I walked over a few feet, to the ladies, and keeping my eyes on the students, I asked what was going on. One of the ladies told me that shooting was going on at Virginia Tech, and the scene was active. Then she asked, "Doesn't your daughter go to that school?" I answered, then in tears, I asked if I could shorten my student's play time, and get the children in; I needed to call my daughter immediately. As a substitute, I had the class for the rest of that day. There was no taking the rest of the day off. I used my cell phone repeatedly to call Christina, but got no answer.

Reaching home, I made several calls to Christina's cell phone, but got no answer. The next day, I took the day off, as I didn't yet know if my child were shot or hurt. I had watched the news that reported that 32 people were killed, and I couldn't rest, not until I hear my daughter's voice. An undergraduate student, Seung-Hui Cho, the perpetrator, was killed among the 32 other students on April 16th, 2007. With 17 other students injured, I was extremely worried. That evening, I was finally able to reach my daughter. I was so very relieved. It seemed as if I had been holding my breath, until I could hear from her. I scolded her for not returning my call immediately, and shared with her what a nervous wreck I was. She told me that the classes she had, at Virginia

Tech, were in the evening, and she wasn't on campus during the shooting. She was working at a job she had, off campus. She also at times worked at Virginia Tech, but didn't have to work there that particular day.

And we know that all things work together for good to those who love God, to those who are the called according to His purpose. Romans 8:28

Boy With a Plane

After substitute teaching for seven years, and working with infants for five years, I had learned to enjoy the challenges of working with young children. At first, the thought of my co worker and I, working in a room with ten infants was too overwhelming, but when I established a routine with the help of my co worker, it was pretty easy. The routine consisted of greeting the infants in the morning, giving them breakfast or a bottle of milk, then playing simple nursery rhymes and children's songs as they played. In the mornings, we read to the children and played games like peek-a-boo, wheels on the bus, and other finger play that young children enjoyed. Before we knew it, the children, who had come into our class at eight weeks old, were crawling, then walking and talking. Many of the children gained a love for reading, and one family, whose children started the Even Start program in our class, had two boys who were reading by the time they were three years old. I was even more surprised when the older boy had read a book on how to potty train his two- year- old younger brother. The older boy was only a year older than his little brother. The family was Hispanic, with the mother being more Spanish speaking.

As all of the teachers and the assistant teachers had professional development to complete, we would from time to time, use the computer to read, then take tests and receive certificates for passing particular courses. Sometimes, this was not enough, and we would have to leave our building for professional development. My boss asked my co worker and me to go to Louisville, Kentucky for more professional development. Neither of us liked flying in an airplane, and I had never been on a plane, and had never planned to get on one. Despite my many days of protesting in the days ahead, my boss ordered plane tickets and made hotel reservations for the two of us. I tried and tried to get out of it, but to no avail.

The night before the trip, after I had prayed and prayed about the trip, I had a dream. I dreamed about a little boy of about five years old. The boy picked up a little plastic toy plane and lifted it into the air. He let the plane fly past his face, and as he moved the plane around, at times he turned it to its side, then straightened it back up. He continued flying the plane until he gently put it down. After the boy put the plane down, the Lord said, "And that's how I will have you." I woke from the dream so confident, I finished packing my suitcase. By the time I was showered and dressed, my co worker was outside waiting in her car, to go to the airport.

We got on the plane, and the pilot and his staff asked who we were as we were seated. We told him, and he said that our boss had told him we were afraid to fly. The pilot said we were in for a treat. The staff returned to the cockpit. As the plane took off, my co worker took Dramamine, and went to sleep, but I couldn't sleep. I had to see what was going on. I braced myself as the plane lifted off. As I gave a sigh of relief, the plane was in the air. Shortly after, the pilot caused the plane to lean to the side, straightened it as he flew a while, then leaned it again to the other side. I thought about the dream, and how the Lord had said He had me. I knew that nothing would happen to the plane. The sound of rumbling under this older plane, nor the turbulence in the clouds excited me, because my confidence was in God. After a lay over, we continued on another plane to Louisville, Kentucky. The trip was pretty uneventful, until the sound of gunfire woke us at about 2:oo a.m. on the morning we had to leave. There was a large wedding party at the hotel, and somehow during the event, a fight erupted.

The plane trip on the way home was comfortable, with very little turbulence in the atmosphere. To my boss' dismay, we had survived the trip without a nervous condition.

Blessed be the God and Father of our Lord Jesus Christ, the Father of mercies and God of all comfort, who comforts us in all our tribulations, that we may be able to comfort those in any trouble, with the comfort with which we ourselves are comforted by God. 2 Corinthians 1:3-4

A Little Helper

I had met many young, as well as adolescent, children in my career in the school system. I had worked with their class, but by the next school year, the children went on to the next grade, and only on rare occasions would I see the child again. When I was a teacher's assistant in prekindergarten class, there was a little girl, who stood out in the class. She was extremely polite, kind, and helpful to the other students. So many times, she didn't need help from the teacher that I had ever noticed, but when other students needed help, she would always lend a hand. When the classroom teacher was out for a couple of weeks, the assistant from the class next door peeked in a few of the students' journals, noticing they were behind some of the students in her class. Her students had begun sounding out words, such that, they could write sentences with the pictures they had drawn. The children in my class were still dependent on writing letters that sounded like the words they were trying to say.

With the teacher out for two weeks, I went home and made index cards with a word on each card to represent the subject, adjective, and verb, so that putting the words together, these young students would know how to construct a sentence. Every day, we went over the words on the cards. The students would form the sentence they wanted to write that day, and drew a picture about their sentence. In two weeks, they were writing sentences. Because we had sixteen students, and many of them needed help reading the cards and writing, Heighley, a very bright four-year-old, would help. When she had finished her work, and there was nothing to do between assignments, she would draw and color beautiful pictures, using colors unlike a child of her age.

The next year, when she was in kindergarten, in a different class, Heighley would stop by in the morning, just to get a hug before class began. She would never forget to say, "Hi," when she would see me in the hall, and always lent a hand when someone needed it. By the time Heighley was in second grade, I worked with children with symptoms of autism. In the gym, for physical education, our autism class would mainstream with the regular class, and boy did I need help. The five children I was responsible for, out of our class of ten, needed help staying in line and doing the routine the other children were doing. My children would constantly get out of their lines, yell for no reason, or sometimes cry. Heighley, being in the gym with our class, would come over to the autistic child, rub his or her back, as if her motherly instincts had kicked in. She would talk to them in such a kind way, they would calm down and join the rest of the class again in whatever activity we were doing. I started rewarding Heighley for her work. I would give her Chik-fil-A cards for $10.00, or buy a sketchbook and markers for her, for all of her help. She would have two other girls her age to help as she did. They would also be rewarded for their help. Heighley's mother had asked me to look out for her little girl, but the truth is, her little girl spent so much time helping me in the class. Heighley would still come by for morning hugs and to see how she could help, bringing a friend from time to time to help her as well. Her dad stopped me in the hall one day and asked why I spoiled Heighley so much. I told him how she had helped my students so much, I couldn't help but bless her. I told him that she was one of the sweetest children I had ever met. One day, when she was in first grade, she came to me and said, "Mrs. Jones, my head hurts; will you pray for my head?" I told her of course I would. With heads bowed, I prayed that her headache went away. After the prayer, I asked her how she felt . She said her head felt better. Later that day, watching her play in P.E., I knew she felt much better.

After a car accident, and a back condition aggravated by my having to constantly hold onto some of the children with autism who wouldn't follow where we were going, it was time for me to retire. The children in the autism class would go on to the next grade, and they would be fine, but I knew I needed to tell Heighley I wouldn't be back the next year, because of retirement. Well, with weeks already gone, and the school year coming to a close, one morning I met Heighley in the hall, looking very sad. I asked her what was wrong. She said, "Why didn't you tell me you were retiring? I heard it from another teacher." As tears rolled down her face, I began to cry as well, although I had tried very hard not to. I told her I just didn't know how to tell her I wasn't coming back to the school. I gave her a hug, and we departed in opposite directions. She was like a little angel God had sent to help me, especially with the challenges of working with children with autism.

I will lift up my eyes to the hills—From whence comes my help? My help comes from the Lord, who made heaven and earth. Psalm 121 1-2

Finally

When I think about a Christian walk, it is one we never do alone. Throughout my Christian walk, despite the things I did unlike a child of God, God forgave me, and continued not only to bless me, but blessed my family as well. God had spent many, many times trying to get me back on a straight path to righteous living.

One day, Jehovah told me: "Behold, I give unto you power to tread on serpent and scorpions, and over all the power of the enemy: and nothing shall by any means hurt you." The word continues and states, "Not withstanding in this rejoice not, that the spirits are subject unto you, but rather rejoice, because your names are written in heaven." Luke 10:19-20

The word of God also states: Then He turned to His disciples and said privately, "Blessed are the eyes which see the things you see; for I tell you that many prophets and kings have desired to see what you see, and have not seen it, and to hear what you hear, and have not heard it." Luke 10:23

A certain lawyer tested the Lord and asked, "Teacher, what shall I do to inherit eternal life?" Jesus said to him, "What is written in the law? What is your reading of it?" So he answered and said, "You shall love the Lord your God with all your heart, with all your soul, with all your strength, and with all your mind, and your neighbor as yourself." And He said to him, "You have answered rightly; do this and you will live." Luke 10:25-28

Jesus equips His children with all they need to successfully make it through this life. He sends His angels, and gives His Holy Spirit to comfort us and to guide us into all righteousness. When we heed God's word from the Bible, as well as heed the warnings when He sends His angels and His prophets for our help and protection, keep His commandments, as well as give tithes and offerings to the church, we have done all we need to stand against the wiles of the devil.

The word of God states, "Finally, my brethren, be strong in the Lord and in the power of His might. Put on the whole armor of God, that you may be able to stand against the wiles of the devil. For we do not wrestle against flesh and blood, but against principalities, against powers, against the rulers of the darkness of this age, against spiritual hosts of wickedness in heavenly places.

Therefore take up the whole armor of God, that you may be able to withstand in the evil day, and having done all, to stand.

Stand therefore, having girded your waist with truth, having put on the breastplate of righteousness, and having shod your feet with the preparation of the gospel of peace; above all, taking the shield of faith with which you will be able to quench all the fiery darts of the wicked one. And take the helmet of salvation, and the sword of the Spirit, which is the word of God; praying always with all prayer and supplication in the Spirit, being watchful to this end with all perseverance and supplication for all the saints–and for me (Paul), that utterance may be given to me, that I may open my mouth boldly to make known the mystery of the gospel, for which I am an ambassador in chains (written from prison); that in it I may speak boldly, as I ought to speak. Ephesians 6:10-20

What then shall we say to these things? If God is for us, who can be against us? He who did not spare His own Son, but delivered Him up for us all, how shall He not with Him also freely give us all things? Who shall bring a charge against God's elect? It is God who justifies. Who is He who condemns? It is Christ who died, and furthermore is also risen, who is even at the right hand of God, who also makes intercessions for us. Who shall separate us from the love of Christ? Shall tribulation, or distress, or persecution, or famine, or nakedness, or peril, or sword? As it was written: For Your sake we are killed all day long: We are accounted as sheep for the slaughter," Yet in all these things we are more than conquerors through Him who loved us. Romans 8:31-37

Many are the afflictions of the righteous, but the Lord delivers him out of them all. He guards all his bones; Not one of them is broken. Evil shall slay the wicked, and those who hate the righteous shall be condemned. The Lord redeems the soul of His servants, and none of those who trust in Him shall be condemned. Psalm 34:19-22

The leech has two daughters–Give and Give! There are three things that are never satisfied, four never say, "Enough!" The grave, the barren womb, the earth that is not satisfied with water–and the fire never says, "Enough!" Proverbs 30:15-16

Go therefore and make disciples of all the nations, baptizing them in the name of the Father and of the Son and of the Holy Spirit, teaching them to do all things that I have commanded you; and lo, I am with you always, even to the end of the age. Amen. Matthew 28:19-20